A GOOD
LIFE TO
THE END

Ken Hillman is a practising intensive care specialist who is a Professor of Intensive Care at the University of New South Wales, the Foundation Director of The Simpson Centre for Health Services Research, and a member of the Ingham Institute of Applied Medical Research. He trained at St Vincent's Hospital in Sydney and worked in London for six years before returning to Australia as Director of Intensive Care at Liverpool Hospital in Sydney. Professor Hillman is internationally recognised as a pioneer in the introduction of the Medical Emergency Team, which recognises and responds to seriously ill hospital patients early in their deterioration and has been adopted in the majority of hospitals in the United Kingdom, the United States of America and several European countries. He is also a passionate advocate of improving   cute hospitals.

A GOOD LIFE TO THE END

Taking control of our inevitable journey through ageing and death

KEN HILLMAN

ALLEN&UNWIN
SYDNEY·MELBOURNE·AUCKLAND·LONDON

Certain names and details have been changed to protect patients' and doctors' identities.

First published in 2017

Copyright © Ken Hillman 2017

Allen & Unwin
83 Alexander Street
Crows Nest NSW 2065
Australia
Phone: (61 2) 8425 0100
Email: info@allenandunwin.com
Web: www.allenandunwin.com

Cataloguing-in-Publication details are available
from the National Library of Australia
www.trove.nla.gov.au

ISBN 978 1 76029 481 6

Set in 13/20 pt Apollo MT by Midland Typesetters, Australia
Printed and bound in Australia by Griffin Press

10 9 8 7 6 5 4 3 2

*This book is dedicated to all the patients and
their caregivers who taught me many things
I couldn't learn from books*

Contents

Introduction   1

1   The last six months of my mother's life   9

2   Ageing is not for the weak   19

3   Because we can, we do   47

4   Falls at the end of life   57

5   Apoptosis   75

6   Groundhog Day   83

7   Cognitive decline   91

8   Denise's manifesto   107

9   Intensive care *sans frontières*   123

10 Diagnostic dilemmas   131

11 Frailty   153

12 It is hard to die   165

13 The living will   175
14 Giving up the ghost   201
15 Futility   221
16 Intensive care: the beginning of the end   231
17 Knockin' on heaven's door   245
18 How to choose a good doctor and a
    good hospital   253
19 The medicalisation of grieving   267
20 The taboos of ageing, death and dying   279
21 Where to next?   289

Acknowledgements   296

Introduction

I have been warned that people will not read a book about ageing and dying as it is too depressing. But death loses its power over us when it is faced matter-of-factly. I believe it would be more depressing to become frail and be near the end of life surrounded by dishonesty and false hope. Knowledge about the true state of our health gives us control over our own life and related decisions.

Anticipating your own end of life lifts the burden from relatives who would otherwise be forced to make crucial decisions about how you should be managed if, for example, you suffered serious brain damage and were destined to spend the rest of your life totally dependent on others. Relatives may make a decision based on reluctance to be seen as uncaring. They may have to live with feelings of guilt, no matter what they decide.

'Hanging on to hope' is sometimes raised during these discussions, followed by clichés such as 'If you haven't got hope then you have nothing left' and similar platitudes. That's fine, if there is real hope, but false hope can be destructive. There may be a place for positive thinking, but not at the expense of reality. People are encouraged to 'fight' terminal cancer, for example, the inference being that if they fail, they are losers. While it's good to be positive and make the most of your life, denying the truth is not doing anyone any favours.

In this book I focus on intelligent pessimism rather than false optimism. Pessimism is not fashionable. Politicians and the media spin the truth in order to paint reality in a more flattering light. Economists are eternal optimists. Medicine reinforces false optimism by only publishing positive results. Optimism is best experienced with a dose of scepticism. That is not necessarily pessimism.

Many of us in western countries will spend their last days in an intensive care unit (ICU). I am an intensive care specialist—an intensivist. My career goes back to the early 1980s. As a specialist in a London teaching hospital, I was attracted by the logic and science of intensive care medicine. I had machines to measure and monitor everything and other machines to sustain life. The potential for prolonging life seemed infinite. I still experience the excitement of saving a life that otherwise would have certainly ended. But I also appreciate the satisfaction associated with orchestrating a good dying process—pain-free, with the patient's dignity intact, and relatives who accept the dying process and are free to grieve in their own way.

Rarely a day goes by when one of my colleagues in intensive care doesn't quietly add a comment along the lines of 'Please don't ever let this happen to me.'

My interest in the issues around end of life has been driven by the change in the population of patients we now manage in hospitals and intensive care units. Once they were relatively young, with life-threatening conditions that were potentially reversible, such as severe infections and trauma. Our specialty made many forms of complex major surgery possible. We now manage patients who have had major cardiac surgery and neurosurgery and who require life support for several days in order to recover. Almost imperceptibly, we began to treat older patients with many age-related conditions. If our machines could save the lives of young patients with otherwise fatal diseases, why not use them on older people? We used to reflect on whether we should be admitting patients who were over seventy years of age after major cardiac surgery. Many survived. Then we were admitting patients who were eighty, then ninety, and I've now managed a few patients who were more than a hundred years old.

Age doesn't necessarily determine survival, but we had overlooked the obvious. Many of the elderly we now treat have the same serious conditions as younger patients, such as trauma and infection, or need care after major surgery. However, their outcome and the course of their illness is determined not so much by these conditions but by the insidious effect that ageing has on the body; the collective accumulation of age-related and chronic conditions such as coronary artery disease, diabetes, dementia and osteoarthritis. When these conditions are combined with the general deterioration in every organ in the body, it leaves the aged vulnerable to diseases such as infection, cancer and even minor falls. All of these factors add up to something that, as yet, hasn't a name or score. Increasingly, we are using terms such as frailty. In fact, we are just beginning to realise that the conditions which bring the elderly frail into hospitals are simply markers of someone who is nearing the end of their life. This is important to note, as it requires a different approach. Instead of admitting the patient to an intensive care unit for the last few days or weeks of life, we could be more honest with patients and their carers about the likely course of their health, allowing them to make choices about how they would like to spend their remaining time.

This book does not present the Walt Disney version of ageing and dying; it is not about how to live longer, how cancer can be cured or how to avoid dementia. Rather, I will be straightforward in my description of ageing, its inevitability and its obvious relationship with dying and death. Like dying and death, ageing is about understanding and acceptance. You cannot accept what you don't know and this book is an attempt to inform.

The patient stories I have shared are based on real situations, though of course clinical details and names have been changed. These stories are not unique to my own experience. The same stories are told in most hospitals around the world. Hospitals are not skilled at recognising and dealing with people at the end of life. They exist to cure people, not to give up on them. Thus I do not intend any criticism of my colleagues. As doctors, we are trained to save lives, not to give in, not to admit that dying is a natural and inevitable part of life. In my professional life, I have had the privilege of working with many dedicated and capable doctors, nurses and allied health practitioners. They are trained to deal with a particular part of the body and they invariably have done so with expertise and care.

The bigger picture, though, is that we have lost the generalist along the way: the family practitioner who suspects that the level of care we provide in hospitals may be inappropriate in view of the overall picture and health of the patient but hasn't the confidence to question the specialists and the daunting technology in big hospitals. The next step is to empower people and community services to care for the elderly frail near the end of life in ways that are consistent with their wishes.

Our passage from the cradle to the grave has become increasingly medicalised, beginning with birthing in the 1950s. Women were admitted to hospitals, where they were strung up with their legs apart, with very little in the way of pain relief, and discouraged from complaining. Their babies were taken from them immediately after birth and put in a large nursery with other newborns. Fathers were excluded from the process, granted only the occasional glimpse into the nursery from behind glass.

The baby boomers then took charge of their own birthing. The same generation is now witnessing their parents suffering prolonged and medicalised deaths in hospitals, with the patient and relatives given little say in what happens. This book is a call to arms: it is time to take charge of dying.

1

The last six months of my mother's life

D r Novak was a Jewish refugee imprisoned in Auschwitz during the Second World War. He looked after my grandfather in the last years of his life, visiting often when my grandfather was ill and finally explaining to his wife, Nellie, and his daughter, my mother Margaret, that he was dying. As a result, my grandfather died peacefully at home in 1959.

There didn't appear to be any fuss and, as far as I could ascertain, my grandfather didn't suffer. My little brother and I were told that our grandfather was dead and was lying in his bed. I don't remember ever hearing about death before. People were sad and my brother and I thought it was all a bit creepy and kept right away from his room. In those days, children didn't go to funerals, but I remember at the wake afterwards the brave faces and funny stories about his life.

Most kids' grandfathers died at home back then. What the family doctor carried in his bag was not much less than what was offered in hospitals. The diagnostic tools, such as stethoscopes, percussion hammers, thermometers, blood pressure machines, otoscopes for looking in ears and ophthalmoscopes for examining eyes were the mainstay of equipment for both the family doctor and for use in the hospital. Hospitals could conduct basic pathology tests and X-rays but the family doctors also had access to these.

The range of drugs was limited—antibiotics, sedatives and pain relief—and, again, these were available in both settings. Only a few surgical procedures were available in hospitals. Anaesthesia could be dangerous and was usually delivered by nurses or junior doctors. Limited surgery was also carried out by the family doctor. I had my tonsils removed under ether on a table in the family doctor's surgery.

Things began to change in the 1960s. The body was divided up by specialists into various '–ologies', such as neurology, cardiology and gastroenterology. Similarly, surgeons began to specialise. The days when the one surgeon performed abdominal surgery, thoracic surgery and a bit of orthopaedic surgery all in the one morning were drawing to a close. Anaesthesia became a separate specialty with the same rigid training requirements as surgical training. This enabled prolonged complex surgical procedures to be undertaken with a previously unknown level of safety. Intensive care units gradually developed in hospitals, facilitating the prolonged and specialised recovery after complex surgery. Other specialties also developed, such as immunology, oncology, geriatrics, palliative care and invasive radiology. Sophisticated imaging and other investigations enabled us to investigate abnormalities with greater accuracy.

It all happened in hospitals, and soon there was a huge gap between what a family practitioner could offer compared to an acute hospital. Hospitals were no longer places where you went to rest while you got better or didn't. They became the self-proclaimed flagships of health care. This was reflected in films at the time. When someone was struck down with an illness or injury in the street, a bystander would shout, 'Quick, call a doctor!' This was soon to be replaced by, 'Quick, call an ambulance!'

My career as an intensive care specialist started a decade or two after the explosion in hospital technology began. Even so, these were early days for the specialty. I was one of the first directors of intensive care to be appointed in London. Those were heady days. I thought the possibilities for prolonging life were infinite. I had life support machines and powerful drugs. My specialty was essential for the complex surgery that was being undertaken. These patients were too ill in the postoperative period to return to the general wards. I could also keep other patients alive while they made themselves better or until our treatment took effect.

In those days, I had six intensive care beds. I now work in a unit with forty beds at a cost of at least AUD$4000 per patient per day. But, it's not just the number of intensive care beds that has changed; it's the nature of the patients we treat. Most of them are over the age of sixty years. Many are in their eighties or nineties. And many of those are in the last few days or weeks of their lives.

My mother, Margaret Hillman, was admitted to a nursing home at the age of eighty-three years, after fracturing her hip. She tried unsuccessfully for one day and night to live independently in her own home but this was not possible. Accommodation was arranged in an aged care institution. She knew this was her only option but was never comfortable living there, despite the excellent care provided by all the staff.

Margaret was cognitively alert until a few days before her death. She had little patience with the other elderly people and thought that if it wasn't for her body physically giving out, she could live a 'normal' life and do 'normal' things.

During the last six months of her life she was admitted twenty-two times to different hospitals for different conditions. She had a urinary catheter inserted at the time of her hip operation and, unfortunately, she could never cope without it. Thus, many of the admissions were for infections of her bladder. Plastic is foreign to the body and when inserted into the bladder or veins, for example, it bypasses the body's first line of defence and makes people prone to infection. The older you are, the more vulnerable you become to infections.

These sorts of infections are easy to treat. For a twenty-year-old with a urinary tract infection it would mean antibiotics and a day off work and then they'd be back on their feet. For an elderly person it is potentially fatal, requiring not only antibiotics but often intravenous fluids and sometimes powerful drugs to support the blood pressure and perhaps admission to an ICU.

Margaret also developed many other problems, including small fractures in her vertebrae, requiring regular narcotics to control the pain. She required a pacemaker and an increasing number of tablets to control blood pressure, reduce cholesterol and to limit her palpitations.

She did not have the same dignified and comfortable death as her father. She suffered despite the pain relief, her mobility declined until she couldn't make her own way to the dining room. She was lonely and sad and she did not want to be continually taken to the hospital.

During this time, I played the role of the son, not a doctor. I didn't want to interfere in any way. Eventually one of the many specialists who had cared for her during her hospital admissions came to see us on her last admission to hospital and explained that she was dying and that to continue to treat her was cruel and to little avail. He said it was time to let her go.

My daughter, Emily, saw her that night and I visited the next morning. Margaret was drowsy with pain relief but still cognitively intact. She died peacefully the next day.

What did my mother die of? Old age. But you are no longer allowed to write that on a death certificate. You need to randomly allocate one of the many conditions my mother had as the cause of death and, similarly, allocate all the other conditions that may have contributed to her death. Because the heart stops when you die, it is common to put the primary cause of death as cardiovascular failure. Hence, it is the most common cause of death in the elderly. When you are elderly and frail you just fade away and your heart stops as part of that fading.

⌒

'What is wrong with me, Ken?' my mother would constantly ask of me in the last six months of her life.

15

Medicine is based on 'the diagnosis', the elusive concept that we spend our undergraduate years learning about. This is relevant if you are dealing with a younger person who has one thing wrong with them. Similarly, hospitals are the perfect place if you have a single diagnosis which can be attended to by a specialist in the offending organ. Unfortunately, this rarely happens—especially in the elderly, like my mother: people who are naturally and normally approaching the end of life and which all the specialists, interventions and tablets cannot cure. This is not to say that we shouldn't care. There are many ways we can support people who are ageing. First, and most importantly, we could begin to be honest about the limitations of modern medicine. Then we could provide things that really matter, such as facilitating the network of friends and family to act as carers; providing real assistance to them; ensuring their house is clean; that they are washed and assisted to mobilise; and that food is provided. These are not medical matters.

It may be better to look at the elderly near the end of life from the patient's perspective rather than dividing up the body into its various organs and giving each age-related deterioration a medical name. The word frailty is becoming useful when describing the sum of all these aged-related conditions. There are many different frailty scores but they all describe in different ways the way age impacts on the body, concentrating on obvious features such as gait speed, the ability to freely move about and look after yourself without help. The concept of frailty is discussed in more detail in chapter 11.

Dying in the elderly has become hijacked by doctors, despite the fact that modern medicine has little to offer. Doctors are programmed to make you better, not to recognise the inevitability of ageing and dying. They rarely feel comfortable talking to you honestly about your prognosis, nor do they empower you to make choices about how you would like to spend the last few months of your life. And even if they did, the funding for community-based care, if that was the wish of the patient, is grossly inadequate. Funding for health is increasingly used to support the sophisticated technology and infrastructure in hospitals—technology that can perform miracles but is often used in a futile way to prolong life in elderly people.

Society needs to demand a different way of doing things and medicine needs to engage society, not only in discussing what it can do but also what it can't do.

2

Ageing is not for the weak

The truth is the older I get, the more I like my defects.
Isabelle Allende, *The Japanese Lover*

You officially become elderly or an older person at the age of sixty or sixty-five, according to different definitions published by the World Health Organization. This figure is arbitrary, not scientifically based.

What is this ageing business all about? While its external signs might be disguised with creams, diets and surgery, behind these, the clock still ticks. The signs of ageing are part of a biologically programmed process which signals that time is drawing to a close for the networks that run our bodies, such as the nervous, endocrine and immune systems. Minor DNA transcription errors accumulate as we age. These occur as small changes in many genes over a lifetime, not large changes in a few genes over a short time. The process is genetically determined and highly variable. The word 'variable' gives us all hope—more hope than anti-ageing creams and Botox. Some people wrinkle, become stiff and go grey early. In others, the ageing process is delayed and they age well. You can't cheat this destiny but you can ensure that you don't shorten your ultimate destiny through environmental abuse such as drugs, a bad diet and lack of exercise.

During your lifetime, you first undergo growth, then reach maturity and finally drift into senescence, or ageing. Senescence doesn't make biological sense. You were born to reach maturity, breed, pass on your genes and then die before you became a liability to your family and tribe. Ageing is a fundamental biological process as a result of apoptosis, or programmed cell death. We'll come to that in chapter 5.

As part of senescence, cells undergo a permanent and irreversible arrest of growth. They change in appearance, accompanied by changes in their DNA and chromosomes. Telomeres are bits of DNA at the end of chromosomes that protect the replicative process and prevent mutations occurring. They are disposable buffers. Some protection for these bits is offered by an enzyme—telomere reverse transcriptase, or TERT. As you age you lose these protective telomeres and your chromosomes gradually shrink. This is sometimes referred to as replicative senescence. The more cellular divisions that occur as you age, the more protective DNA you lose. This is a finite process. As it occurs the telomeres shorten and this largely defines ageing. The cells wear out and cease to be able to replicate effectively. As a result, your appearance and function deteriorate.

The skin is a good place to start when studying ageing. Clive James, the Australian television columnist, translator of Dante and great observer of life, suggests that the first sign of ageing is wrinkling of the skin at the back of the elbow.

Skin holds you together. It also helps to control your temperature; helps fluid and electrolyte balance; and contains nerves to detect temperature, pain, pressure and pleasure. It consists of three layers: the epidermis, made up of skin cells and pigment; the dermis, containing blood vessels, nerves, hair follicles and oil glands; and the third and deepest layer: the subcutaneous layer which contains sweat glands, blood vessels and fat. Each layer also has connective tissue, with collagen to give support and elastin fibres to give elasticity.

The epidermis thins with age; the number of melanocytes or pigment cells decreases in number but increases in size. Thus you become paler and more translucent. Large pigment spots, called 'liver' or 'age' spots, become common. The first sign of my own ageing was the appearance of a small, pigmented area on the inside of my foot behind the ankle bone when I was twenty-five. I was horrified!

The connective tissue in every layer decreases as we age, reducing elasticity and strength, a process known as elastosis. In people exposed to the sun over a lifetime, such as farmers, the elastosis produces a leathery appearance.

Blood vessels become fragile, which can lead to bruising. There are fewer oil-producing glands, resulting in the skin drying out. The subcutaneous fat decreases, making you susceptible to cold, while the loss of sweat glands makes you more susceptible to heat. All sorts of other blemishes, such as skin tags and warts, become more common. The appearance of your skin is also related to your body water content. The body consists of 80 per cent water when you are born, about 60 per cent in your thirties and 40 per cent in your eighties. You dry out as you become older. Granny's skin is different from a newborn's in obvious ways. Because you comprise less water as you age, you don't need to drink as much. One of the few advantages of ageing is that, compared to babies, you are less prone to dehydration.

Skin wrinkling—often considered the first sign of ageing—is a natural result of decreased elastin and collagen as you age. Wrinkling can be hastened by repeated muscle activity, such as around the eyes, as well as by smoking, sun damage, poor hydration and weight loss. Botox works by paralysing the muscles that can make wrinkles less prominent. Avoidance of smoking and direct sunlight might decrease the onset of wrinkles. Surgery may temporarily stretch old skin, but it will not influence the inevitable ageing of skin. Nor do creams stop the ageing process of skin. Chemicals are rarely absorbed through the skin, especially large and complex molecules such as collagen and serums. They just sit on the skin and eventually are washed off. That's money down the drain.

Let's turn to your hair ... Remember, hair is dead—thus, it doesn't require nutrients. Ignore ads for products that promise to make your hair more alive. No matter what chemicals you put on it to make it shine or give it bounce, it is still dead. With ageing, the pigment called melanin, responsible for hair colour and produced by hair follicles, decreases. Greying often begins in the thirties. This is genetically determined and nothing, apart from dye, will decrease its rate.

Each hair will last about two to six years and this is also genetically determined. As you age, the rate of growth does not keep up with hair loss. Hair strands become thinner and have less pigment. Many hair follicles stop making hair. This is biologically logical, as you don't need to remain attractive because your breeding role diminishes as you age. You will also lose facial and body hair, and the hairs that remain become coarser, especially around the chin and lips in women and around the eyebrows, ears and nose in men.

Your nails grow more slowly as you age and they become duller and more brittle. They may even become yellow and opaque.

The kidneys do not age gracefully. They weigh about 50 grams at birth, reach a maximum of about 400 grams by your forties and gradually shrink to about 300 grams if you reach ninety. The kidneys contain millions of little filters, called glomeruli. They filter out waste products such as creatinine, acid and urea, and precisely regulate electrolytes such as sodium and potassium. The ability to filter decreases, beginning in your twenties. The number of glomeruli decreases and the ability of the remaining ones is compromised as they become leakier. They are reduced to about half of their original number if you reach eighty. The vessels supplying the filters become sclerotic or hardened, also impairing renal function.

The urine you make is then passed into the bladder via two ureters, one from each kidney. The bladder becomes less stretchy as you age. It cannot hold as much, meaning more night trips to the toilet. The muscles controlling the bladder weaken, which means you are more likely to leak and dribble. Even without an enlarged prostate, men will still suffer from an ageing bladder. (One of the advantages of a free market economy is its ability to adapt to the times, so while I notice there are an increasing number of anti-ageing commercials, there are also more promotions for pads for the elderly to cope with those 'little embarrassing moments'.)

The liver is a powerhouse. It has multiple roles, including making bile; synthetising proteins for important functions such as clotting; storing energy supplies; sorting out how many nutrients need to be manufactured and where they are to go; and detoxifying our own dangerous chemicals, as well as metabolising drugs such as alcohol and all the other medications you may collect during the ageing process. The liver is the only organ, apart from the brain, that I can't support in one way or another in my intensive care unit. There is no liver equivalent to renal dialysis.

So what happens to it as we age? It gets much smaller and turns brown—so-called 'brown atrophy'. It secretes less bile. The liver's blood supply is reduced to about half its size by the time you reach sixty. This limits its housekeeping ability. By the time you are around eighty you have half the number of liver cells you had at forty. The remaining cells often show signs of ageing. At ninety, the liver is half the weight it was when you were thirty. Much of the liver is replaced by fat as it ages. In other words, it ages badly and becomes much less capable of doing its work. Importantly, you can tolerate less alcohol. An enzyme, alcohol dehydrogenase, is made by the liver cells. The amount made decreases as your liver shrinks and the cells are not replaced. Your hangovers become worse. Maybe some smart entrepreneur will add alcohol dehydrogenase to the wine, enabling you to keep up with the younger ones. On second thoughts, that might impress the other drinkers but it would defeat the purpose of drinking the alcohol as there would be less available to share its pleasurable effects. On third thoughts, it could mean the end of the elusive hunt for manufacturing the best wines with low-alcohol, without diminishing their beautiful tastes and aromas.

Your olfactory system, or sense of smell, also deteriorates as you age. Images of corpulent men enjoying fine wine, cigars and food are erroneous. Their sense of smell and taste has been considerably reduced. You also become 'long in the tooth' as a result of the gums retracting, not because the teeth get larger.

The system you have for processing food also declines. Starting from the top, your tongue becomes weaker; your teeth, if you still have them, aren't as efficient; and the swallowing muscles at the back of your mouth don't work in their normal coordinated way to provide a clean and efficient swallow. The gag reflex, sensing food going down the wrong way, is absent in about 40 per cent of elderly people. Even food that makes it to the bottom of the gullet or oesophagus may be delayed in its passage into the stomach. Sometimes the food that does make it into the stomach is regurgitated as a result of a weak sphincter between the oesophagus and stomach, resulting in the so-called gastro-oesophageal reflux disease (GORD). It is not surprising, therefore, that you are at increased risk of aspirating food and liquid into your lungs, predisposing to pneumonia. That process is accelerated in those suffering dementia and is a common cause of their eventual death.

You may also suffer from post-prandial hypotension or blood pressure drop as a result of the blood supply being diverted to the gut after eating, leaving insufficient blood flow to important organs such as your heart and brain. Thus, you may become dizzy after eating and perhaps suffer a fall.

The nerves supplying the gut decrease and become less efficient as ageing occurs. The gut may become more sluggish, with a higher incidence of constipation. It is not uncommon for the abdomen of the elderly patients in intensive care to become distended as a result of gas accumulation. This is partly due to the sluggishness of the gut but also due to the fact that the patients are ill and are often nursed on their backs. It is very difficult to pass gas while the weight of your body presses on your anus up against the sheet. We sometimes have to administer a drug that stimulates the bowel into action and at the same time turn patients on their side and stand back.

It may get even uglier towards the end of the bowel. The functioning of your rectum and anus deteriorates. Rectal sensation and anal tone decreases, possibly accounting for the unwanted passage of gas and faecal incontinence and telltale skid marks on your underwear.

Towards the end of your life you begin to lose weight and waste away—the anorexia of ageing. There are many possible reasons, including decreased sense of smell and taste as well as an early sense of satiation due to structural changes in the stomach and the abnormal secretion of hormones. Perhaps there are other factors, such as general weakness and lack of interest, and the fact that the body's metabolism has slowed down and doesn't need as much fuel.

Apart from the skin, your posture becomes an obvious marker for ageing. Bones decrease in mass and density, becoming more brittle and more easily broken. They become decalcified, especially in women and as a result of decreased exercise. The spine, in particular, is affected as it becomes more curved and compressed. The joints or spaces between the vertebrae also decrease, as a result of which you become shorter. The foot arch grows less pronounced, reducing your height even more. However, your arms and legs remain the same length, giving the appearance of being longer.

The joints between the bones degenerate and produce less fluid. Thus the cartilage rubs together and erodes, increasing degenerative changes. Minerals can be deposited in the joints, especially the shoulder joint. As a result, you begin to creak with age. Pain on movement becomes greater. Some joints, such as the hip and knee joints, become so damaged that they may need replacing. The joints become inflamed and stiff. Osteoarthritis and rheumatoid arthritis become more common. A once simple task, such as alighting from a car or getting up from your chair, becomes an effort. It takes a while for things to start working again from a standing start or in the morning.

The muscles also suffer with age. The changes, known as sarcopenia, result in a decrease in size, number and composition of muscle fibres. I call it the 'Lufthansa syndrome', because I first noticed it when, at about the age of fifty, I was alighting from a Lufthansa aircraft down those mobile steps they wheel up to the plane. I was carrying a heavy bag and found that I had to hold on to the rail as my quadriceps were giving way. It's been downhill since. Slowly, incrementally, I'm holding on to more rails and avoiding sitting on the grass as it's too difficult to get up.

The rate at which muscles atrophy or waste, depends mainly on your genes but also on caring for your body with exercise and weight control. The muscle fibres not only decrease in number but they shrink. Lipofuscin (an age-related pigment) and fat are deposited in muscles. The muscles gradually lose their tone and become more rigid. We all prefer to eat the muscles of young chickens rather than old 'boilers'. Some muscles waste earlier than others, such as the ones in the fingers, making them look longer and bony. Particularly repugnant to women is the sagging of the triceps in the upper arm.

So, as we have seen, you will become shorter, more stooped and your hips and knees will become more flexed as they lose their ability to straighten. In addition, the neck becomes tilted, the shoulders narrower and the pelvis wider. You will become more unsteady; your gait will become slower and shorter; and you will tire more easily as the strength and endurance of the muscles decrease. Small twitchings of the skin, or fasciculations, will become more common, and sometimes you will suffer pins and needles, or paraesthesia. You are heading for a walking frame or even a wheelchair.

As you become weaker and your balance becomes impaired, you have an increased risk of falling. Hospitals assess this risk and take measures to prevent it. The avoidance of falls is one of a hospital's performance indicators. At one hospital where I worked, they confined patients to bed in order to improve performance, knowing that while the risk of falls decreased in the hospital, the immobility would increase muscle wasting and bone demineralisation at an even greater rate.

The impairment of sight may contribute to the likelihood of falls. Light first enters the eye through the cornea, then travelling through the lens, which focuses the image on the retina at the back of the eye. This image is carried by the optic nerve to the very back of the brain, where you register sight. It is a beautiful and complex system in which each component is essential for accurate sight.

I first realised I needed reading glasses when I tried to read a street directory one night in the dim light of a car. (I didn't mind. I thought reading glasses perched on the end of my nose would make people take me more seriously!) I had developed presbyopia—I was losing the ability to focus and read small print, and holding the text further away and squinting didn't help. Presbyopia usually begins in your forties. There are other age-related problems with sight. The lens in your eye no longer focuses precisely on the retina, causing a scattering of light, creating glare. You develop subtle changes in colour perception. As tear production dries up, eyes may feel drier.

Floaters and flashes due to particles in the eye fluid are a natural part of ageing. However, age-related macular degeneration can be particularly debilitating. Cataracts and glaucoma are also more common with ageing. Cataracts are a result of the lens clouding up and becoming less pliable. The cloudiness diminishes the vision and the lack of flexibility interferes with your ability to focus on fine print. The clouded lens or cataract can be surgically replaced.

Here's something else to look for as you age—arcus senilis: the arc of old age. It is usually a white or grey opaque line around the cornea appearing as a circle around the iris or coloured part of the eye. It usually starts at six and twelve o'clock and spreads to form a circle. It's yet another sign that you are not getting any younger.

Sight is not the only sense affected; as you age, all your senses deteriorate, including hearing. The ears perform two roles: hearing and balance. Hearing is as a result of your eardrum or tympanic membrane transmitting sound via three very small, delicate bones connected to your brain by a network of nerves. Age-related hearing loss is called presbycusis. It results in a diminishing ability to hear high-frequency sounds and the inability to distinguish sounds, especially when there is background noise (which explains why I am having increasing difficulty hearing those opposite me in restaurants or at parties). The message is: don't invest in expensive sound systems as you age; you won't be able to tell the difference.

Thousands of tiny hair cells pick up sound waves and translate the sound into nerve signals in the inner ear, from where they are transmitted to the brain for you to register and interpret. Hearing loss occurs when the small hair cells die or are damaged and not replaced. Like most things, the degree and onset of loss is mainly related to your genes but can be made worse by factors such as repeated exposure to local noise, disease or drugs.

From the intricacies of sight and sound, let's turn to the 'big-ticket items'. The heart and lungs are among the so-called 'vital' organs. They provide the cells of the body with the oxygen and nutrients necessary for life. The heart pumps blood into the lungs where it picks up oxygen, then back to the heart where it is pumped around the body. During this journey oxygen is offloaded to the tissues, and then veins carry blood back to the heart to be pumped into the lungs for another load of oxygen. Nutrients are picked up on the way back to the heart from the intestines and liver. And so the blood goes around and around your body, from your time in utero to the moment when the heart stops and the circulation ceases—in other words, death.

Your circulation becomes poorer as you age. The walls of the capillaries abutting the cells thicken. Unfortunately, this is where all the action occurs in regard to the exchange of gases and nutrients and, as such, the exchange can gradually become less efficient and the circulation slows. However, most of the changes occur in the walls of the arteries, especially the major one: the aorta. It takes the full pressure from the heart with each beat. It's not surprising that with these continuous pressure insults come changes, known as 'hardening'. The aorta and, to a lesser extent, other arteries become stiffer as a result of the walls becoming more rigid, made worse with cholesterol deposits and eventually with calcium deposits, causing the aorta to resemble bone. This process is also known as arteriosclerosis. It is a normal part of ageing, but with a medical name. It develops to different degrees and at different times, determined mainly by genes but also influenced by environmental factors such as smoking and diet.

Because the arteries become hardened, they are less elastic and cannot accommodate the pressure changes that occur with each heartbeat. The heart has to work harder as the pressure needed to force the blood from the heart has to increase in the face of the hardened arteries. Smoking especially accelerates ateriosclerosis, raising the blood pressure. The arteries of a smoker not only become harder, they narrow until there may be insufficient blood flow, especially to the legs, which, as a result, sometimes require amputation.

The thickening of the arteries is inevitable with age no matter how healthy a life you lead. And so is the increased pressure needed to pump blood into the hardened arteries. Obviously, if the pressure is too high, organs at the end of that high pressure, such as the kidneys, brain and eyes, suffer. Many elderly people are on blood pressure tablets which can delay or even prevent strokes, as well as slow deterioration in the functioning of the heart and kidney. However, the pressure requirements increase as you age. You don't want elderly patients becoming dizzy and falling over every time they stand up as a result of the blood pressure not being high enough to keep the brain perfused.

The heart also suffers as a result of the increasing pressure. The walls have to thicken and increase in strength to maintain the higher pressure. As the strain increases, the heart can become larger and the pump begins to fail. Scar tissue also forms in the struggling heart, which makes it stiffer and less able to relax after each pump. It is therefore less likely to fill adequately in order to provide the next pump. The heart struggles to pump out adequate amounts of blood (called systolic failure) and struggles to relax and fill after each pump (called diastolic failure). This results in the gradual failing of the pump and is an important contributor to the process whereby ageing begins to merge with dying.

The symptoms of heart failure include shortness of breath, swollen legs, tiredness and a decreased ability to exercise. The coronary arteries supplying the heart also suffer as a result of their narrowing and the increased work in maintaining the pressure necessary to pump blood around the body. Of course, factors such as increased cholesterol, diabetes and the clots which finally block the narrowed and hardened arteries also cause decreased cardiac function and heart attacks.

Scarring in the heart also affects the nerve conduction system which controls regular heartbeats. The scarring can also lead to calcium deposits in the heart valves, especially the aortic valve. Not surprisingly, it is often referred to as senile aortic stenosis and may need repair.

Many of these pathologies are largely contributed to by the irreversible effects of ageing, rather than separate diseases that can be cured. The ageing heart is a fertile area for the medical and pharmaceutical industries. A failing heart may be related to blocked coronary arteries, requiring coronary artery surgery to unblock them. Increasingly, cardiologists are doing the same things with safer, less invasive procedures. Anticlotting agents, such as aspirin and more expensive options, help to prevent blocking of the arteries; a pacemaker keeps the heart beating; drugs control arrhythmias and blood pressure; drugs prevent strokes when the arrhythmias occur; other drugs lower your cholesterol. A huge industry has been built around the deterioration of the heart and circulation.

On the other hand, you don't hear much about the ageing of lungs. Well, not as much as the ageing of the heart, skin, bones, muscles, joints and brain. Perhaps it's because the lungs only become important towards the actual end of life. Like many organs, your lungs mature in your twenties and from then on deteriorate. As they become less efficient and the cough becomes weaker, secretions tend to accumulate, eventually becoming infected, causing pneumonia—'the old man's friend', a painless and gentle way to leave this earth.

The 'death rattles' are due to the inability to cough sufficiently to clear secretions and they just rattle up and down with each breath. The 'rattles' can also come about as a result of water on the lungs as the heart fails. The lungs become less efficient due to a combination of bone changes in the rib cage, the weakening of the muscles responsible for breathing and actual changes in the lung itself—all combined with a decreased ability of the lung to fight infection.

The ribs become thinner and stiffer, making the rib cage less able to expand and contract during breathing. As the spine shortens, the lungs are compressed into a smaller space. The muscles that pump the lungs up and down, especially the diaphragm, become weaker and contribute to your decreasing ability to exercise, contributing also to your tiredness and shortness of breath.

The lung tissue also changes with age. The alveoli, where gas exchange occurs, become baggy and lose shape, leading to 'senile emphysema'. This condition is exacerbated by the loss of supporting structures within the lung parenchyma. On top of all these changes, the ageing lung is unable to resist infection as well as when you were younger.

This means you are not able to take the large breaths you could when you were younger; increasingly, you cannot generate the same force to blow out the birthday candles. The rate of decline is variable, but can be as much as a 70 per cent decline by the age of eighty compared to the age of twenty. It's the same old story—the rate of deterioration is largely genetically determined but made much worse by environmental factors such as smoking. Many eighty-year-old smokers are confined to a chair, unable to generate enough breath to stand up.

The voice is tied up with the lungs. The failure to generate strong airflow rates makes the voice sound weaker. This is made worse by weakened laryngeal muscles, reducing the range of sounds and giving the voice a higher pitch.

And, finally, let's talk about sex . . . The ageing of genitals cannot be looked at in isolation from their major function—sexuality. Males and females should probably be discussed separately for obvious reasons. Sexuality in itself has to be looked at in the broader context of its components, such as the genitals, hormones, nerves, psychology and social environment.

We know that frequency of desire, erection and intercourse decline with age, but this is variable and related to many issues, such as general state of health, concurrent diseases and social context.

Sticking just to the anatomy, a woman's vagina shortens and becomes narrower. The walls become thinner, the clitoris atrophies and there may be less lubricant. Very few women over the age of forty can conceive, no matter how sexually active they are, and their eggs have deteriorated to such an extent that it is usually impossible to use them for IVF programs.

Most elderly men have some cancerous changes in their prostate and most, when they finally die of something else, have some degree of prostate disease. Men become more impotent. By the age of sixty-five, about one-fifth of men have this problem at times. The erection may not be as firm and the amount of ejaculate may be smaller. There are many other age-related factors occurring at the same time, such as arthritis, less muscle strength, dementia, and concurrent medications and illnesses. Of course, this is further complicated by the nature of the relationship and the social and cultural context as well as the psychological make-up.

⌣

As I mentioned at the start of this chapter, we were not meant to grow old. In evolutionary terms, we were born with the simple aim of surviving childhood, reaching adolescence and very early adulthood, passing on our genes and then dying—like the salmon returning to spawn at the height of their physical development and then dying. Most great athletes are at their peak in their twenties; you are competitively over the hill for most sports by your mid-thirties.

You start ageing in your twenties, making you more vulnerable to disease, trauma and various environmental tribulations. However, due to advances in medicine and public health, you are cocooned through middle age into old age. I'm seeing more of you in my ICU on life support machines at the end of your life. There are times when I can delay the immediate threat to your life, such as if you have fallen off a ladder or suffered a urinary tract infection. However, it can be distressing when a colleague rings me and says, 'I have someone who needs your help. He's ninety-five but a *good* ninety-five-year-old.'

There is no such thing as a physically good ninety-five-year-old. He may have been doing odd jobs, helping to care for the grandkids and great-grandkids only the week before; and, of course, he is dearly loved and respected by all who know him. However, his reserve has run down, so that he no longer has the capacity to survive even minor insults, such as pneumonia. As with most situations in medicine, there is uncertainty. Uncertainty is combined with pressure from colleagues, unreal societal expectations of medicine, grieving and anxious families and our own medical training to 'cure' patients. The result is that we probably give people false hope and are not honest about the chances of their surviving, at what emotional cost survival may come, and, even if they were likely to leave hospital, what type of quality of life they would have in their remaining weeks or months.

Even acknowledging uncertainty, we could begin discussing 'non-beneficial' or futile medical treatment. This would include concepts such as death being imminent; where treatment would have no effect;

where the patient would be unlikely to survive without the support of machines in an ICU; honestly discussing the patient's goals and determining whether these could be met; whether the burden of treatment far outweighs any benefit. Clinicians often overestimate the benefits of their treatment and underestimate its harm. We need to move to a patient-centred approach rather than choices being limited by short-term medical goals.

Most elderly people are not given a genuine choice about how they want to live their remaining years. Usually, the fact that they have little time left is not even discussed. And yet there is data which gives us some idea of the likelihood that you may have less than a year or two to live.

Creams and plastic surgery do not delay the ageing process. Medications and some surgery, such as joint replacements and coronary artery grafting, can improve the quality and even length of life, and healthy living may help you to live to your maximum potential—but none of these things will help you to live past it. Nothing stops the ageing process.

3

Because we can, we do

Cardiac surgery requires complex teamwork. Most surgery is aimed at grafting the arteries supplying the heart that have become blocked, usually over many years, as a result of a combination of bad genes, ageing and lifestyle. There are other ways of unblocking the arteries, such as administering 'clot-busting' drugs, which dissolve the blockage, or 'non-invasive' procedures, such as stenting the artery by squashing the clot against the vessel wall. Another option aimed at slowing the progression of heart disease is using drugs that inhibit further clot formation.

Cardiac surgeons can perform miracles and many patients feel a new lease of life after arteries supplying the heart are unblocked and blood with a fresh supply of oxygen is supplied to a heart muscle starved of it for many years.

However, it is not always the case that improved heart function improves the patient's lifestyle. While many patients feel like a new person, others are no better off and some are in fact much worse off. Of those who survive the operation and the hospital stay, many have such severe pre-existing damage to the heart that there will be little improvement. Others suffer complications and/or the debilitating effect of such major surgery combined with long periods on life support in an intensive care unit.

The standard recovery plan from cardiac surgery covers approximately eight weeks, if the right patient is chosen for the right operation at the right time and all goes well during the hazardous hospital journey. You are told that you may not feel yourself for a while. You may experience a bit of pain in the chest on coughing and laughing. Instructions are given for wound care. An exercise program is recommended, as are lifestyle changes. You are advised to avoid salt.

As for sex: 'Be caring, honest and loving with each other.' Uh-oh! This doesn't sound promising—but at least you are alive.

I can imagine an advertisement marketing the operation. The kindly surgeon in a white coat, smiling benevolently, explains the procedure to a fit-looking man of no more than sixty. His slightly anxious-looking wife is at his side, listening attentively. This is followed by a long shot of the man in intensive care, again with his wife sitting next to the bed. Cut to the ward, where he is seen taking a few tentative steps. In the final shot, the health professionals are waving goodbye as he leaves the hospital with his smiling wife, and the pair drive off into the distance.

Cardiac surgery has changed and will continue to change. Cardiologists are picking the low-hanging fruit with their drugs, stents and balloons. Like video rental shops, you could see it coming. There are not so many applicants for the cardiac surgical training program these days. There is still a place for cardiac surgery, but it's often limited to complex operations on elderly sick patients for whom, in many cases, the surgery shouldn't have been contemplated in the first place.

This has been a bad week. Maybe I'm just tired, but my ICU colleagues share my concern.

The man in bed 18, Mr DeWitt, has been in intensive care for over four weeks. He is extremely weak and can barely move following a long, complex cardiac operation. Mr DeWitt had four coronary arteries grafted and one of his valves replaced. He previously had his bladder removed—it was cancerous—and replaced by a piece of his small intestine fashioned to function as a bladder. Unfortunately, the cancer has spread and he has metastases in his lung. Because of his bad heart he was too sick to have the chemotherapy necessary to control, not cure, his metastases. So he had major cardiac surgery so that he would be well enough to live through the palliative chemotherapy.

The operation went badly. Mr DeWitt lost a lot of blood and had a cardiac arrest. He required extracorporeal membrane oxygenation (ECMO), one of the most sophisticated technologies we have in intensive care, to keep him alive after the operation. ECMO takes over the function of the heart and lungs. He also needed an intra-aortic balloon pump (IABP), another complex bit of machinery that assists hearts that just aren't up to the job.

Three weeks later he has woken up and has a tracheostomy. He is on a ventilator and needs continuous dialysis because his kidneys never regained function after the operation.

The lady next to him, Mrs Norris, is not doing much better. In fact, she is where Mr DeWitt was three weeks ago. She has all the so-called co-morbidities, or other medical problems that often accompany heart disease—diabetes, hypertension, obesity and high cholesterol. Despite this, she had major heart surgery: four coronary artery grafts. Her heart couldn't function by itself after the operation and still can't one week later. As a result, she is on ECMO, has an IABP, is on industrial doses of drugs to maintain her blood pressure and on continuous dialysis because her kidneys, which were not good in the first place, took a hit.

Mrs Davenport looked like she would do better. After the operation her heart was working and her lungs were good. Unfortunately, she didn't wake up and the CT scan showed a massive haemorrhage in her brain from which she will never totally recover. Discussions with the family are underway.

Let's try to reconstruct the events surrounding the outcomes for these three patients in case you are ever caught up in a similar situation. After they have established you have heart disease that may be amenable to cardiac surgery, the cardiac surgeon will have a family meeting with you. They will focus on the problem at hand, such as the blocked artery or malfunctioning heart valve—which, in theory, they could readily fix. They might advise that unless the problem is fixed you will become worse and may die. This could be true and is presumably why you would consent to the procedure. It would have been hard for the cardiac surgeon to say anything else—except, perhaps, to put the option in the context of the patient's whole life. Because we have so many short-term options for so many problems, we utilise them. This is incremental medicine, fine-tuning bits of the body, patching things up with little regard to where the patient is ultimately headed. The cardiac surgeons, like most medical specialists, tend to explore their own bit of the body. It's a bit like a panel beater recommending that extensive damage to the side of the car be repaired when the motor is about to seize up irretrievably.

Individual choice or autonomy is, of course, important. But the patient's ability to exercise it depends on how the choice is put—if, in fact, a choice should be offered at all without also explaining the overall health status of the patient and the context of the proposed intervention. A choice offered without all the facts is not really a choice; it's a foregone conclusion. It's a rare doctor who doesn't operate from a single organ or specialty perspective; who considers the body as a whole; who discusses quality of life and how choices may impact on even small procedures; who understands the interaction of the various medical conditions and, finally, offers people genuine choices about how they want to spend their remaining years and in what state of health.

⌐

It was a cold, rainy Saturday morning—the sort of weather I love. There was no pressure to enjoy the outdoors; instead, I drove through the rain to see my patients. I can't pretend it's because I'm virtuous or doing this for humanity; I feel privileged to have a job that I love.

It's hard to distance oneself from fellow humans' suffering, especially if you feel that you can alleviate that suffering. The woman in bed 4 was suffering.

Brought up in Ireland by a gypsy grandmother, she was quite a character. Now sixty years of age, she was morbidly obese, and had undergone cardiac surgery for blocked coronary arteries six months ago. The arteries were unblocked but the heart never really functioned any better. She was in rehabilitation for five months, making no progress, with no hope of returning to an independent life in her own home. Now she was in my ICU having massive infusions of drugs to keep her blood pressure up. The heart had failed even more since the operation and now it wasn't functioning well enough to sustain her life. As a result, her kidneys had shut down. The renal specialist did not want to dialyse her because her heart would not recover to the extent that would eventually restore function to them.

I spoke to her cardiologist, who said her most recent tests of cardiac function were good and that it wasn't the heart that was causing the problem. Rather than raise the dangerous subject of dying, I reported that I had tried stopping the drugs supporting her heart and her blood pressure had dropped. It didn't appear to me that her heart was ever going to support her body. The cardiologist insisted her heart was functioning well and we should continue to actively treat her. I pointed out that as he considered her heart to be normal, it should be able to function without the drugs. It was a circular discussion, going nowhere. And in fairness to my colleague, he firmly believed, like most doctors, that he was doing his best to keep his patient alive.

Despite her serious state of health, the woman in bed 4 was conscious and alert, supported by the drugs. I started discussions with her by asking if anyone had spoken to her about her lack of progress after the operation and the seriousness of her current condition. No one had. I explained her poor prognosis. She decided she wanted to leave hospital and go home. Both of her children had been suggesting this long before she had the operation.

I passed this on to the cardiologist, who refused to accept that she was dying. I went back and explained to the woman that her doctor thought she should stay in hospital. I ceased some of the drugs and transferred her to a ward under the care of her cardiologist, where she quietly and painlessly passed away twelve hours later.

The same Saturday and I was waiting for the transfer of a patient from the operating theatres after an urgent operation to unblock her coronary arteries.

The woman was eighty years of age, demented, with significant renal impairment and has had a form completed, stating that in the event of her having a cardiac arrest, resuscitation would not be attempted. And now, because we could unblock her arteries, we did. The almost certainly terminal condition of the patient was disregarded. We had something we could fix and so, damn it, we fixed it.

The relatives agreed to the operation. This was another case of choices being based on limited and distorted information. They had signed the consent form after the situation was explained something like this: 'Your mother is very ill. She has blocked coronary arteries. Her only hope is surgery. What do you think?' There were many other ways the situation could have been explained and they could have been offered other choices. For example: 'Your mother is very ill. She has blocked arteries. In view of her underlying condition, we don't believe surgery would be safe or successful. What do you think she would have liked?'

She died on a life support machine three days later.

Sometimes it is not the long hours my job demands that exhaust me so much as the frustration of trying to balance what we could do against what we should do.

4
Falls at the end of life

Falls can be trivial and fatal at the same time. The patient in bed 1, Reg Flinders aged seventy-three, fell while putting his pants on. He had probably had a bit too much to drink, as happened on most nights since his wife died six months ago. He got tangled up in his pants and, after one or two hops, went straight down on his left side. Luckily his daughter was just dropping some meals off for him to heat up over the next few days and heard the crash.

Trapped on the floor by his recalcitrant pants, he was struggling to get them over his ankles. When his daughter asked if he was okay, he assured her he was fine. The daughter gently slipped his pants off but, as she moved him, he began to moan from the pain across the left side of his chest and upper abdomen. Despite his protestations, she called the ambulance. While waiting for it to arrive, she put a new pair of pants on her father and also packed a few bathroom things, his tablets, a pair of pyjamas and his dressing gown—little knowing that nurses and doctors in emergency departments are annoyed when a patient arrives with their personal things in a bag, as it offends their right to make the call as to who is admitted to their hospital and who is sent home.

Fortunately, the admitting doctor was aware of the possible complications the elderly can suffer as a result of falls. Fractured hips in the elderly have mortality figures similar to untreatable cancer and other end-stage diseases. Fractured limbs, particularly hips, are usually obvious by the appearance of the leg and they can cause excruciating pain. Many patients are now admitted for urgent surgical reconstruction— with pins, plates and a variety of screws. Fractured ribs are usually not amenable to surgical intervention. They heal by themselves over a few weeks.

The doctor immediately administered strong intra-venous pain relief to Reg and continued the assessment.

He had multiple fractured ribs on the left lower side of his chest. These are life-threatening in an older person, especially if they smoke, which Reg did until two years ago. Now he just drank.

Until relatively recently, surgeons did not allow pain relief to be given to anyone presenting to the hospital as it could mask the patient's signs and make it difficult for doctors to make a diagnosis. But the pain caused by fractured ribs, especially on deep breathing or coughing, can cause further problems. Small breaths and no coughing results in the lungs not fully expanding and, as a result, they begin to collapse. Sputum begins to accumulate in the collapsed part of the lung. They then become wet and heavy, which in turn makes it more difficult to breathe. As a result, more of the lung collapses, which, together with the pain from the fractured ribs, makes it even harder to breathe; so more collapse occurs, eventually resulting in a lack of oxygen and sometimes even death. This is unlikely in young patients, because they have reserves, but in older patients, fractured ribs are a common and lethal condition.

The ageing patient has an increased risk of falls. The muscles and bones become weaker or more brittle;

the heart may cause blackouts because of a transient palpitation; the multiple drugs and decreased ability to metabolise them may cause dizziness; and the normally deteriorating brain, combined with confusion, may contribute to a lack of balance.

I treat about twenty males over the age of sixty-five each year in the intensive care unit after they fall off ladders, fracturing their ribs. Interestingly, they look their best when first presenting to the emergency department. Many used to be sent home with inadequate pain relief and died. We are now more aware of the potential complications in the elderly, and patients with fractured ribs are either admitted to the general wards or directly to the ICU, depending on factors such as their age, history of smoking, previous health and the number of ribs fractured. Patients who have the same ribs broken in two places are particularly vulnerable. The segment of broken ribs between the two breaks is sucked in when the patient breathes in, instead of being held securely by the ribs. As a result, the lung around this so-called 'flail' segment is particularly prone to collapse. The lung next to the broken ribs may also be bruised, which can exacerbate the problem. So the older DIY-ers who insist on climbing ladders are often admitted directly to the ICU after a fall. Copious pain relief is given and the lungs are ventilated in order to prevent them collapsing. The positive pressure is usually delivered via a mask.

In Reg's case, this was not enough to prevent further collapse and he had to be artificially ventilated, the air delivered by a plastic tube inserted directly into the windpipe. Reg's blood pressure dropped suddenly about forty-eight hours after he was admitted to hospital. After excluding any complications involving his heart or a clot in his lungs, an abdominal CT scan showed that the impact over the ribs had caused his spleen to rupture. He was rushed to the operating theatre, transfused with blood and had his spleen removed. Apart from its involvement in dealing with particular types of infection, the spleen is one of the organs you can live without.

Reg's medical course was now going to be complicated by the pain of the operation as well as the fractured ribs and blood loss. In anticipation of a longer and rockier course, a tracheostomy, or incision in the neck to accommodate the plastic tube to his lungs, was performed at the same operation.

After a further two weeks, Reg had his tracheostomy tube removed, and two weeks after that, he left hospital. All this was the result of being elderly and tripping over his pants while getting dressed. Ageing makes us more vulnerable to even the simplest of insults such as minor injuries or infections.

⌐⌐

June Winter was in bed 7. She was eighty-four years old and fell in her bedroom. She had fallen on the right side of her head. June was living with her son and his family. Her daughter-in-law found June on the floor, confused and disorientated. The daughter-in-law called the paramedics, who arrived within a few minutes. On examination, June was found to have a swelling on the right side of her head, almost certainly blood causing extensive bruising. The Glasgow coma scale (GCS) measures the level of consciousness. A score of three is the lowest, indicating there is no response at all, and fifteen is normal. June had a score of seven. This was not good, but she was still responding to the outside world, although very drowsy.

The paramedics rushed her to our emergency department, where she was immediately intubated—a tube was inserted into her windpipe—and placed on artificial ventilation. Soon after, a CT scan of her brain showed a subdural haemorrhage. The dura lines the brain. A haemorrhage can occur outside the dura, where it is called an extradural haemorrhage, or under the dura but outside the brain, known as a subdural haemorrhage. The blood clot or haematoma was compressing the underlying brain. A subdural haematoma in an eighty-four-year-old has an extremely poor prognosis. Removing the blood clot, which seems intuitively logical, has little impact on the outcome. The problem in medicine is translating statistics into action. Should the compelling figures suggesting a poor outcome translate into doing nothing? At least by removing the clot, the already damaged brain would not be compressed by the clot. The neurosurgeons—who, in my experience, hold out more hope in otherwise hopeless situations than almost any other specialty— decided not to operate. I explained her poor prognosis to the family, but to be more certain and to give the family time to assimilate the news, I suggested we rest her brain for forty-eight hours and assess her level of consciousness then. If she remained unconscious, but was breathing by herself, then we would take her off the respirator and see how things went. However, if she was to deteriorate, we would not escalate treatment.

At forty-eight hours we took her off the respirator; the GCS remained at three, but she was still breathing.

We had just moved into our new ICU, which had a special room to manage patients who were dying. There may have been other units in the world with similar facilities but we did not know of any. Our staff designed this one specifically to manage patients at the end of their lives. The room was large, capable of holding many chairs for friends and relatives. There was an en suite bathroom, coffee- and tea-making facilities, a sink, kitchenware and a view through large glass doors. The management of dying patients changes from supporting life to supporting the dying patient, ensuring there is no pain or suffering and that the patient is treated with dignity. Management of the dying also involves care of the relatives and friends. Even when there is no hope of recovery, it is important to make it clear to the relatives that we continue to care for their loved one, albeit with different management goals. For example, a nurse does not have to be there all the time. Intensive care nurses sometimes find it difficult to change the goals of care, as their usual role is to be alert to the many things that need to be done to sustain life.

It was the first time I had managed a patient in our 'special' room—it is difficult to know what to call it, as all the euphemisms still meant that it was the room where we cared for patients at the end of life. The room was as I had imagined: a special room where patients could die with dignity and where their loved ones were able to be involved and share those moments in privacy and with a sense of being cared for.

June died peacefully eighteen hours after we removed the ventilator.

⌒

Emily Donaldson was eighty-five years of age. Her family had been discussing the possibility of a nursing home with her as she was having increasing difficulty getting around. This was despite her apartment being fitted with rails in the bathroom and ramps replacing the stairs and many other adjustments in an attempt to make the home safe. She had ceased driving five years ago after a minor accident when her foot became tangled somehow on its way to applying the brakes.

Emily had many of the underlying problems common to eighty-five-year-olds, including a failing heart. This only had a minimal impact on her lifestyle, as her mobility and ability to exercise was severely limited by arthritis and diminished muscle strength and, as such, she did not require a good heart to get around. She also had high blood pressure, high cholesterol, diabetes and coronary artery disease, or narrowing of the vessels supporting the heart.

I rarely come across patients over the age of eighty years in the ICU who have not got at least a couple of these age-related problems. Emily's cognitive functioning was pretty good, but she stumbled over a gutter while walking to the shops and fractured her hip. Approximately 15 per cent of patients with a hip fracture do not survive hospital and about one-third are dead within a year. Up to 80 per cent never return to their pre-fracture ambulatory state. It is not so much the fracture that accounts for the poor prognosis as the fact that falling and osteoporotic bones are both markers of how close one is to the end of life.

The paramedics were fantastic, arriving within minutes of being called by a passer-by and were immediately aware of what had happened without even having to touch her: the injury as a result of a fall, her age, the agonising pain made worse by the slightest movement and the telltale shortening of the injured leg with the foot turned outwards. Convinced she had fractured her hip, they explained what had to be done. They administered pain relief in the form of syrup, spray and pain-relieving gas, which allowed them to put her on a stretcher with minimal discomfort and move her to the ambulance.

The operation she later had involved putting metal hardware through the fracture in the neck of the femur. The neck is the thinnest part of the femur. It joins the shaft of the femur—the longest bone in the body—with the ball on the end of the femur, which in turn fits neatly into the pelvis. Emily, like many women of her age, was also osteoporotic as a result of decalcification of her bones.

Two days after the operation, she developed pulmonary oedema or fluid on her lungs as a result of a minor heart attack on the background of a heart already not pumping well. An urgent call was made and resuscitation began. She had to be put on a life support machine and was taken to the ICU for artificial ventilation. Large intravenous catheters were inserted into her veins and powerful drugs given to support her circulation.

The incremental creep of medical interventions had started. She came in for a simple orthopaedic procedure. These days, the technical aspect of the procedure is straightforward and relatively uneventful; simply inserting a metal pin in order to stabilise the fracture. The real challenge would be getting Emily back on her feet and out of hospital. The co-morbidities, or background medical problems, and Emily's age posed the real threat to her recovery. And now one of her already narrowed coronary vessels had blocked off completely, causing a heart attack and cardiac dysfunction. The heart could not effectively pump her blood around the body; the blood had built up in her heart, causing back pressure, which resulted in fluid on her lungs. Because of the cardiac dysfunction, Emily's kidneys were also beginning to suffer. Dialysis was being considered.

Emily could not be involved in the conversation, as she was sedated heavily. Her son suspected she would not like a prolonged death with potential suffering if the outcome was so grim. I tried to explain how there was almost never certainty about these things but it was looking less likely that she would survive. He asked the obvious question: 'Well, how likely?' In terms of odds, I estimated she had less than a 20 per cent chance of recovery. If her kidneys failed, her chances would drop to less than 5 per cent. No one has the exact figures and every patient is different in terms of age, resilience, co-morbidities and the nature of the sudden deterioration, but that would be a rough ballpark figure.

Next came the difficult bit. If her kidneys failed, I could dialyse her. In America, I would offer the son choices—supermarket medicine. I could continue to ventilate her; I could dialyse her; if the heart got worse, I could put her on extracorporeal membrane oxygenation (ECMO) and support her heart and lungs until they recovered. If neither the heart nor kidneys recovered, in theory I could offer transplantation. Many of these options are only mentioned to indicate how far modern medicine can go in order to sustain life. The more complex ones would not be offered, even in the United States. However, some of the less invasive ones may be offered, especially in a country like the United States, where a perverse incentive is inherent in all medical decisions—you are paid for doing more, each 'item', each procedure you do, each extra day in hospital has a price tag and that is how you earn your living. That is what pays the mortgage and college fees. The lesson: do not undergo prolongation of life support in a private setting.

This is the approach I took: I said to Emily's son that while there was always uncertainty in medicine, why not leave her on the life support machine and see what happened. 'Although it is unlikely,' I told him, 'she may have the strength to get over this setback.' I did not offer dialysis or even mention it as an option. If I was to say that dialysis would keep his mother alive and without it she would die, and then asked her son: 'What do you think we should do?', there was really only one answer he could give. In my opinion, this would have been a cruel and expedient approach, as there was no mention of the fact that she would be highly unlikely to survive her experience in the ICU. It would simply be a matter of prolonging her life with drugs and machines with no prospect of recovery. I do not believe this is the role of intensive care.

By offering choices, it appears that the doctor is being inclusive and caring. On the other hand, they are not being honest about the eventual outcome and the unnecessary suffering of the patient and family by offering false hope. When the patient eventually dies after several more days or weeks, they can reassure the relatives by saying: 'We gave her every chance.' The doctor and family are absolved of any guilt.

The motives for doctors avoiding honest discussions about dying may just be that they have had little training in the area or maybe that they consider medicine *is* about prolonging life at all costs. I also know that many of my specialist colleagues appear to be uncomfortable discussing dying. Perhaps it comes from a feeling of failure. In which case, they are considering their own needs over those of their patient and the patient's family.

The challenge is to achieve consensus about treatment without asking permission. In Australia, we are not too sure if Emily's son has the right to demand everything that western medicine has to offer. We are not too sure if even the patient has this right. But we do know that the surrogate's choice—in this case, the son's—does not necessarily coincide with the patient's. And is the son likely to refuse dialysis? The response could largely be determined by how the question is framed rather than by ethical rights and wrongs. 'We could dialyse and give her a chance.' Or, 'There is dialysis, but I don't think it would work for your mother.' Or, 'Dialysis is an option, but I don't believe it would influence your mother's chances of recovery one way or another and it is likely to add to her suffering in the final days of her life.'

As the patient's kidneys were still functioning, although compromised, I chose not to mention the possibility of dialysis. I would leave that discussion for the time being, as many other complications might occur in the meantime which would make the decision to dialyse clearer. So I explained that her kidneys were failing but they might turn around.

Within three days, Emily's lungs had cleared, but her kidneys never regained their function. She died four days later.

In those people aged eighty-five years or older, half of all women and a third of all men will have significant falls in the community each year. It is approximately three times higher for those in the same age group who are in institutions. Falls account for about 10 per cent of all visits to emergency departments and, of those, about the same percentage are admitted to hospital. Nearly 20 per cent of all admissions to the emergency department for those over sixty-five are for falls, and of these half require admission to hospital.

I am treating an increasing number of men over the age of seventy years who fall off ladders while continuing to do minor repairs around the house. Some of these die and most spend at least three or four days on high level support in an ICU. Maybe it's time to conduct public awareness campaigns or perhaps to issue ladder licences to those aged over seventy!

There are many strategies to reduce the incidence of falls—give up climbing ladders when you reach sixty years of age; maintain a healthy weight; exercise, especially the lower limbs; redesign your home to limit risks; minimise the intake of drugs that cause drowsiness; and use the many different types of devices that aid walking safely.

However, many of us as we age will still end our lives or have severely diminished mobility as a result of a fall. It is just what happens.

5

Apoptosis

We are short-lived reincarnations. Every one of our
billions of atoms has almost certainly passed through
stars and been part of millions of organisms, including
other people, on their way to becoming you.

Bill Bryson, *A Short History of Nearly Everything*

It begins at the moment of conception. The combination of the mother's and father's genes will determine how your body will age—the timing of your natural death and disintegration of cells; the deterioration of your tissues; and the gradual failure of all the networks and communication between tissues and organs.

The genetically programmed death was dramatically emphasised for me when I was caring for an eighty-six-year-old woman who died of a severe infection.

Infection is often the cause of death in the elderly. They just lose the strength and immunity to fight the infection. When we tried to contact my patient's twin sister, we found that she had died from a severe infection in another intensive care unit on the previous day.

Apoptosis is the process of programmed cell death. The word 'apoptosis' is Greek in origin and refers to the 'dropping off' of petals or leaves from plants. It does not involve external factors. Your cells are programmed to die; you will gradually decompose and melt back into nature, re-emerging as other forms of life.

Dying cells display molecules on their surface, indicating that they are ready to sacrifice themselves. As the cell destroys itself, bits of the cell disintegrate and fragment and the cell shrinks. Many pathways and signals can cause the cell to undergo apoptosis.

After internal disintegration, the remnants are marked for mopping up by roaming executioner cells called macrophages. The macrophages operate quickly and silently to engulf the dying cell before it spills out its contents, causing surrounding chemical damage. Using special instruments, you can see the engulfed cellular fragments in the macrophages as they go about their business.

When the number of cells undergoing apoptosis is excessive, it leads to atrophy, wasting or certain disease states. At other times, insufficient control of the cellular balance causes proliferation, such as in cancer. Sometimes cancer can result from faulty cells being able to replicate rather than being mopped up by apoptosis. Other disease states can cause excessive and unregulated apoptosis, such as in the case of HIV, where lymphocyte cells produced in the bone marrow die at an accelerated rate through uncontrolled apoptosis.

Life is about continual regeneration and destruction of your cells. It is estimated that up to a thousand billion cells die each day in an adult human as a result of apoptosis. This is balanced by the continued replication of existing cells by a process known as mitosis or cell division. The process of apoptosis occurs together with mitosis. The balance varies according to the different stages of your life. Mitosis outnumbers apoptosis in children and young adults, resulting in growth. In late adolescence things even out. Then the grim reaper takes over. Loss of cells becomes greater than the production of cells and your skin begins to wrinkle and your muscle bulk decreases. Like something out of a science fiction movie, you begin to devour yourself.

But let's not get too excited; apoptosis is essential for life as we know it. For example, in the foetus, the cells between the fingers and toes undergo apoptosis, allowing the digits to separate. Similarly, after birth, apoptosis is essential to maintain body integrity and vitality. Having reached their 'use-by' date, cells have to be removed.

We are just beginning to learn about the dying process. For example, there are enzymes, or specialised proteins, in the cell, called caspases. They help to orchestrate programmed destruction by attacking and cleaving the structural proteins inside the cell. They exist throughout the animal kingdom and are an integral part of the evolutionary grand plan. The caspases selectively slice and dice bits of their own cells. It is not a wholesale demolition. You are carefully carved up from the inside.

There is a second set of proteins crucial to cell suicide, the Bcl-Z family. Some of this family advocate a death sentence and some advocate life. They continually interact with each other. When pro-death family members are more numerous, a sentence is passed and the execution begins.

Another part of the cell, the mitochondrion, also plays a role in this process. It is the cell's powerhouse, but also its arsenal, containing many of the killer proteins released when the Bcl-Z family gives the go-ahead.

Apoptosis ensures that you were not designed to live forever. At least, not in the physical sense. You were designed to breed and then die. The apoptotic process is held in check until you become a breeder, sometime in adolescence and early adulthood. Then apoptosis takes over. You gradually begin dying from within. Your hearing and eyesight become impaired, muscle bulk decreases and so does cognitive function. Humans used to die in our twenties or thirties. This was not the result of a massive apoptosis event. (In fact, apoptosis is rarely the direct cause of death.) Rather, the gradual decline made you more vulnerable to external threats such as predators, disease and accidents. You couldn't run as fast or keep up with the tribe.

However, many of us, particularly in the developed world, now live a cocooned life. We are guaranteed food without having to hunt or cultivate it. Most of us have a roof over our heads. The temperature in our homes is regulated. Public health measures such as clean water and sanitation have decreased the risk of infection. And then there are the miracles of modern medicine: drugs to control our naturally increasing blood pressure; chemicals to control our diabetes, ensuring that we live to pass on the defective genes to our progeny; drugs to lower the cholesterol; procedures to keep the coronary artery vessels open; interventions to remove tumours. We cheat the apoptotic process and move into a state of old age. The development of intensive care units has guaranteed that you not only live until you are literally falling to pieces, immobile and demented, but that you can be kept alive even beyond that point with life support machines, complex machinery and strong drugs. Evolution never anticipated the development of ICUs.

Some people see natural ageing and dying as the next challenge for medicine to overcome. Already commerce and academics are beginning to identify the triggers for apoptosis—not out of scientific curiosity but to profit from the natural instinct of the privileged few to cheat ageing and death. It is highly likely that anti-apoptosis units will blossom, perhaps targeting certain tissues, such as skin, brain or muscle bulk. At the same time, the majority living in developing countries will succumb early to starvation, disease and trauma.

No matter how much we tinker with the natural ageing and dying process, though, biology will eventually win. Some will survive longer than others; everyone has a different genetic make-up. We all age at different rates. Some people are living in a rapidly deteriorating body by the age of thirty, while others have been programmed differently. And, of course, you are more likely to reach your apoptotic potential with a good diet and plenty of exercise. However, the tiny time bombs in each cell will gradually result in the total collapse of your body, mowing down the last stragglers who manage to avoid its inevitable consequences. Inherent in the beauty of life is death.

6

Groundhog Day

Human kind cannot bear very much reality.

T.S. Eliot, 'Burnt Norton'

I'd just returned from a few weeks' leave over the Christmas period. At the initial handover at 0800 on the first morning I couldn't help but wonder: 'What am I doing here?' Maybe, because of the break, I was able to stand back and watch the ritual of the handover through fresh eyes. And it seemed unreal. Almost all of the patients in the unit were within days or weeks of dying. Instead of being at home, surrounded by loved ones, they were on machines, surrounded by well-meaning healthcare workers who were focused on keeping them alive.

The handover in intensive care involves exchanging details of each patient: the age of the person, the reason for admission to the ICU, the progress they have made, the current situation and possible future directions. I have been trained to concentrate on making this person better, not to question the whole business. But that's exactly what I was doing.

Luciano, in bed 1, was ninety-four years old and had been in the ICU for twelve days after undergoing an extensive operation to remove his prostatic cancer. Almost every ninety-four-year-old man has some cancerous change in his prostate and most, with or without cancer, no longer have the robust urinary stream of a twenty-year-old. What were the gains for him?

The extensive surgery simply exposed his age and lack of reserves. The excessive blood loss during surgery didn't help. He was so weak now he could barely move. He hadn't the strength to breathe and we hadn't been able to wean him off the ventilator. His hands were tied to the bed to prevent him pulling out the paraphernalia that was keeping him alive. He couldn't talk because of the tube going between his vocal cords and into his lungs. I decided on my first day back that I would probably take him off the ventilator the next day. I would make sure both he and his family understood everything we were doing and why. I would reassure them that whether he pulled through or not, he would not suffer any pain or discomfort. At least he would be able to talk to his family before he died.

Cyril, in bed 2, was only sixty-six years old. He had smoked almost all his adult life and was confined to a chair at home as he hadn't enough functioning lung left to sustain any movement. He was exhausted at rest. Cyril had suffered an episode of bronchitis bad enough to tip him over the edge. He was rushed to hospital, where an oxygen mask was put on to assist his breathing and he was given antibiotics. He was now almost well enough to be discharged home into his chair. I asked him if he wanted to come into hospital next time he suffered a setback or if he would prefer to stay at home and be given drugs to diminish the awful sense of breathlessness. Without hesitation, he said he did not want to come back into hospital and could not understand why they just wouldn't let him die in peace. I promised I would arrange the appropriate support in his home and that we would ensure he would not suffer any pain or breathlessness.

Francesca was in bed 3. She was only sixty-two years old and had end-stage multiple myeloma. This is a cancer of one of the body's white cells—the plasma cells, which are responsible for immunity. The cells can accumulate in the bone marrow, interfering with production of other blood cells. The cells are also responsible for the accumulation of proteins in the blood which can block the kidneys, interfering with their function. Multiple myeloma is almost never curable but can respond well to treatment, especially in the early phases.

However, Francesca had had the disease for many years and now only had days or, at most, weeks to live. She had severe electrolyte disturbances and her kidneys had almost totally failed. It had been decided that she would not be suitable for dialysis as she was close to the end. Francesca was totally aware of her surroundings and not in any way cognitively impaired.

Two days earlier she had asked why, if she was soon to die, was she brought into hospital and admitted to the ICU? The team explained that the electrolyte disturbance could be easily treated and that had been successful. She continued to push for explanations and suggested that if she only had a few days or weeks to live, she would prefer to be at home with her family rather than in a hospital, cared for by strangers. She couldn't see the point in aggressively treating one symptom when the disease itself and other complications were untreatable. Like many patients, she hadn't been given choices about her treatment. It wasn't until the renal failure became an issue that open and honest discussions began.

Clive, in bed 4, was admitted from a nursing home. He had become drowsy and developed a fever. An ambulance was called and a urinary tract infection diagnosed in the emergency department. From there, because the infection was life-threatening, he was transferred to the ICU. These infections are easy to treat for intensivists—resuscitation with intravenous fluids, drugs to sustain the blood pressure and antibiotics. Most get better.

Clive had severe dementia and was unable to move from his bed in the nursing home. He had suffered recent weight loss and, despite good care, was developing pressure sores. He was seventy-seven years old and had the all too common list of other age-related health problems: chronic kidney failure, coronary artery disease for which he'd had heart surgery, diabetes, high blood pressure and high cholesterol. Although his urinary tract infection was treatable, it was hard to see the sense in curing him just to have him transferred back to the nursing home bed to see out his last few weeks or months of life, bedridden and totally dependent on others for all his needs. None of us involved in his care would have wanted that for ourselves. But Clive hadn't expressed his wishes one way or another while able. And doctors are programmed to do things, not just sit back and consider the overall picture.

Fifty-two-year-old Daryl, in bed 5, had literally drunk himself to death. He was barely conscious, having suffered severe damage to his brain as a result of his liver not being capable of metabolising the toxic poisons in his blood. Despite full life support, Daryl had not improved over the last two weeks. He was deeply jaundiced and had a grossly swollen abdomen from liver cirrhosis and ascites, or excess fluid in his abdomen. After the ward round I would talk to the other specialists involved in his care and the family with a view to withdrawing active treatment.

We then came to Ivan in bed 6. He was seventy-seven years old, had severe dementia and was being looked after by his wife. He had fallen down a flight of five stairs and was brought in by ambulance last night. He was conscious but confused—this was probably a result of his dementia, but there was a very small chance that he also had a brain injury as a result of the trauma. He was sent for a CT scan to determine if this was the case. Thinking it through, though, I could not imagine too many doctors would propose emergency neurosurgery on a seventy-seven-year-old, severely demented man.

The CT scan showed a small amount of blood in Ivan's brain—not symptomatic but almost certainly as a result of trauma. The next step was to admit him to the ICU in order to observe him in case the bleeding became worse. The obvious problem with this was that he almost certainly would not be considered for surgery even if he did deteriorate.

There was another issue too: Ivan's wife was seventy-five and could not cope anymore with the full-time care of her husband, even before the fall. She needed a lot more support in the home or Ivan needed to be cared for in a more appropriate community setting. But that sort of community resource is scarce whereas, in spite of their cost, acute hospitals are available at any time of day or night.

This issue of cost not only applied to Ivan but to the other five patients I've described. Caring for them in hospital was costing society over AUD$4000 per patient per day, as well as giving caregivers false hope and causing suffering to patients. It was a lose–lose situation.

Finally, there was good news when the ward round reached Alexander in bed 7. We had a patient with a potentially treatable condition who, if he survived, could be discharged from hospital alive. Alexander was seventeen years old and had been diagnosed with Guillain–Barré syndrome. The syndrome results in gradual paralysis of muscles, including the diaphragm, which meant Alexander couldn't breathe adequately and was on a ventilator. He was a young person with a life-threatening illness. Without the expertise and resources of an ICU he would not live. The disease would run its course over a few days or weeks; he would then no longer require any support and would be discharged home to live a relatively normal life.

The specialty of intensive care was originally established to treat exactly this sort of illness. How then did our specialty become one where much of our effort was devoted to support patients who were naturally and predictably at the end of their lives?

7
Cognitive decline

When we hear the word 'dementia', we automatically think of Alzheimer's. While this is the most common form of medically classified dementia there are many other causes of dementia. In this chapter, we will concentrate on age-related cognitive decline, which can lead to symptoms similar to and even the same as medically classified dementia. These include a decline in memory or other thinking skills, which can compromise a person's ability to perform everyday activities.

Both age-related cognitive decline and other forms of dementia are currently incurable and both can cause a lot of suffering, especially for the caregivers. Medicine has a tendency to tidy up conditions into diagnoses. We avoid saying that the problem is simply a part of ageing. Nevertheless, dementia is related to ageing. It has an incidence of less than 5 per cent in people between the ages of sixty-five and seventy-four, and up to 50 per cent in people over the age of eighty-five years.

Authorities have tried to modify the connotations associated with the emotive word 'dementia' by assigning a different term for the elderly: age-related cognitive deterioration. As part of the normal ageing progress, there is deterioration in some functions such as short-term memory, processing time and reaction time. Other functions, such as knowledge, may increase. Characteristics of cognitive decline related to ageing, include:

- It is inherent in all humans and, indeed, other animals as they age.
- It occurs in all individuals as they age, regardless of their initial cognitive function.
- It is a dynamic and highly variable process between, and within, individuals.
- Some cognitive functions may improve, decline or not change and there is the potential for older adults to strengthen some cognitive abilities.

- It is not a neurological or psychiatric disease and does not inevitably lead to the same degree of nerve cell death and degeneration present in other forms of 'medical' dementia such as Alzheimer's disease.

In other words, to a lesser or greater extent, this cognitive decline is normal and a natural part of ageing.

Cognitive decline as a result of ageing is not easy to pin down, even with the many assessment tools we have. There are no blood tests for diagnosing dementia of any sort, although it is the subject of active research groups around the world. Similarly, there are no specific changes identifying cognitive decline in ageing in any of the imaging we have, no matter how sophisticated it is. Moreover, the cognitive tests that we use are influenced by many factors, such as education, cultural background, health and occupation. Currently, the best way to assess cognitive decline is by analysing changes over time. There is no exact point at which you can assign the diagnostic label of age-related cognitive decline. It seems we just gradually drift there in much the same way as the rest of the body ages. Like all other aspects of ageing, there is variability in the timing of its onset and the degree of cognitive impairment. There are some people who remain intellectually prolific until late in life, whether through working to maintain brain function, their genes, their diet, their environment or other factors. Richard Strauss was in his mid-eighties when he wrote his *Four Last Songs*. German baroque composer Georg Philipp Telemann was still writing beautiful music up until the evening of his death on 25 June 1797, aged eighty-six. Irish writer Edna O'Brien completed her masterpiece, *The Little Red Chairs*, in her nineties. There are many more examples.

There are things you can do to slow or prevent dementia, whether it's 'medical' or age-related, such as avoiding smoking, excessive consumption of alcohol and head trauma, maintaining exercise and controlling blood pressure.

However, the picture remains confused. For example, there is evidence that some patients with obvious cellular damage in the brain that is associated with dementia have relatively unimpaired cognitive function, while others with considerable cognitive impairment had relatively few of the cellular changes associated with dementia. This lends hope to the importance of other preventative factors, such as exercise.

However, apart from avoiding ageing, for the time being beware of catchy phrases such as 'boot camp for the brain'. The idea of maintaining 'brain fitness' through board games, learning a new language and doing crosswords has captured the public's attention, but there is no evidence to suggest these methods are successful.

I look at many CT scans of the brain in the course of my professional life. The images of the brain of those in early adulthood are packed with brain cells, with a minimum amount of the fluid that cushions the brain during normal activities. As we age, there are fewer brain cells and more fluid. The brain shrinks. It is not a subtle feature. It is an obvious and universal feature. Some older patients appear to have less than half the brain matter of younger patients. This loss of cells is consistent with the slow degeneration of other organs, such as the liver and kidney. What is more difficult to determine is how to correlate the obvious decrease in brain volume with a reduction in cognitive function.

The brain also functions differently throughout our lifetime. That makes sense. A child has a lot of learning to do. Children become fluent in languages without much effort. The fifty-year-old who decides to learn

French before the annual holiday struggles, however, and most people will barely become fluent even with a lot of effort. The brain of a fifty-year-old has lost that ability. The brain of an adolescent is different again. It is also learning at a rapid rate. The owner of that brain has to leave home soon and fend for themselves. Their brain begins to challenge all previous learning and instructs its body to take risks and experience new challenges. It no longer sees the parents and authority figures in the same way. When a parent chastises a teenager, they often ask: 'What were you thinking?!' Well, for a start, the teenager wasn't thinking like the parent. The adolescent's brain sees things differently from the adult one. The generation gap is partly a result of people having different brains at different times, equipping them to adapt to different challenges at different stages in their lives.

The older brain cannot learn as quickly as it once did, and as a result is no longer prepared to take risks. The older brain cannot imagine what its own younger form was like. When older brains get together, they reminisce and imagine a world where they didn't behave outrageously. They are disdainful of the need for adolescents to behave in a collective way, forgetting that they once conformed to their own peers, even if that involved early sexual activity, risk taking and the excessive use of whatever drugs were around at the time. Many see their own adolescence as a blissful period where they were a well-behaved individual who just drifted seamlessly into adulthood without breaking rules or causing trouble.

The older brain can become predictable and repetitive. Perhaps you can exercise your brain to avoid this: stop relating the same old stories; don't complain about other drivers on the road. Instead of being predictable in your interpretation of world events and reinforcing the way your ideas may have become fossilised, work on your curiosity and open-mindedness. For example, bring a different perspective to the way events are reported in our media: who are allies and why? Who are the criminals in our society? Research the political party you've supported all your life. Do a bit of reading; think a bit laterally. Shock and impress people with your new and insightful interpretation of things.

Typical manifestations of age-related cognitive decline include memory loss; forgetting which word to use or struggling to find the right words; losing things; developing inflexible ways of operating and irritability when routines are disrupted; disorientation; and needing help with new technology. Day-to-day functions can be affected, such as working through complex financial issues, understanding instructions about your health and driving. More serious features include becoming irritable or behaving inappropriately. Many people suffer agitation and frustration when they have problems performing simple tasks and they have a fear of losing control—when threatened with having their driver's licence taken away, for example.

Deterioration over time is the most accurate way of distinguishing between age-related cognitive impairment and some of the more serious forms of dementia. In the latter stages of dementia, whatever the cause, some become restless and begin to wander. A 'catastrophic reaction', such as fear or anger, can occur suddenly when the sufferer is put in a situation beyond their understanding or capabilities. A common symptom is to deny that relatives, even immediate ones, are members of their own family. Being unable to perform tasks such as bathing, dressing and walking without assistance marks severe dementia. A loss of independent mobility usually denotes survival for no longer than six months. Other features of severe dementia include urinary and faecal incompetence, and the inability to speak or communicate meaningfully. This usually means that speech is limited to half a dozen or fewer intelligible words in the course of a day or during an interview. Finally, difficulty swallowing, refusal to eat and weight loss are features of terminal dementia. Advanced dementia is a terminal disease like many forms of cancer. However, there is significant variation in the presentation and progression of dementia. In the latter stages, you will usually not directly die of your brain failing and lapsing into a coma; you will die of related factors, such as your brain not controlling your swallowing and coughing enough to prevent pneumonia. You may acquire a urinary tract infection or suffer a fall. Even the most obsessive care by others may not prevent these complications as you deteriorate.

While there may be some promising drugs currently undergoing trials, particularly in the early stages of dementia, the bad news is there is currently no cure, whether medical or related to age-related cognitive decline. People with dementia are often seriously neglected while we encourage an all too willing public to spend millions searching for the cure rather than adequately supporting the sufferers and their carers. None of the extensively studied potential cures have worked. This hasn't stopped medical experts using phrases such as 'are routinely prescribed' or 'should be considered' when discussing these unproven treatments. This is in spite of the serious and sometimes life-threatening complications that can accompany such drug usage, especially in the elderly.

In anticipation of declining cognitive function, you may want to consider some pre-emptive action. Imagine you have severe dementia and that you contract a disease such as pneumonia, which is not only potentially fatal but also potentially treatable. If, under these circumstances, you wouldn't want to be aggressively treated, then talk to those you trust and formalise it in a living will or as part of advanced care planning (see chapter 13). While you are thinking about a life with dementia, also formalise your financial affairs. Appoint an enduring power of attorney, someone who can carry out your instructions when you may not be of 'sound mind' and your decisions could be challenged or ignored. 'Elder abuse' is becoming more common around the world. As dementia worsens, you may be prone to financial exploitation. It may be an idea to have an open discussion with your family about your financial wishes before they are formalised so that future confrontations and family rifts are minimised.

Apart from the elusive search for a cure, how should we manage people with dementia? First, by acknowledging that cognitive decline is a normal part of ageing, like the skin changing as we get older. That may help to decrease the stigma and confusion that is sometimes associated with dementia. We should also make it clear to our families that if serious dementia were to cripple who we are, we may not want potentially treatable medical conditions to be actively managed, especially if it means being admitted to acute hospitals and undergoing aggressive life support in an intensive care unit.

We could also be more honest about the prognosis and course of severe end-stage dementia, which would help family members and other carers understand just what is in store for them and their loved ones. Even severely demented patients may live up to one or two years. Survival time largely depends on the existence of other medical conditions and the comprehensiveness of care.

We can also address the problem of how to appropriately support the increasing numbers of patients and carers whose lives are severely compromised by dementia in all its forms. This may not be as glamorous as finding a cure but it is of crucial importance to patients and their carers.

Most importantly, we could divert some of the huge levels of funding currently devoted to finding a cure for dementia and instead focus on determining the most effective and evidence-based way of providing support for the sufferers and their carers in order that they might live with quality and dignity. This would do more to ensure the burden of care is shared by our society and not by individuals. In contrast to society's willingness to pay almost obscenely large sums of money for new medical technology and drugs, those who are paid to care for the elderly infirm are on equally obscene low wages—or, in the case of family caregivers, are unpaid.

The problems facing caregivers was illustrated for me by the case of George and his wife Lorraine. George was sixty-seven years of age and had been caring for Lorraine at home since she developed early dementia eleven years ago. Lorraine had been admitted to hospital four times over the last twelve months, twice with a life-threatening urinary tract infection and twice with life-threatening pneumonia. On each occasion, the symptoms of the infection were recognised early by George and he rushed her to hospital. Twice she was admitted by the renal physicians for her urinary tract infection and twice by the respiratory physicians for the pneumonia. On each occasion, the correct treatment was delivered. It's not complex—a barrage of investigations, followed by intravenous fluids and antibiotics. What is more difficult, and what is not in many textbooks, is the contextual aspect of treatment.

Lorraine had severe dementia. She couldn't bathe or dress alone; she couldn't walk without assistance; she needed to be fed; she was incontinent of faeces and urine; and she couldn't speak in an under-standable way.

Despite well-meaning social workers, George did not receive coordinated support in the community. Four different government departments were involved with her support. It took George many months—and the help of friends and a network of people facing similar challenges—even to discover their existence and ascertain their respective roles.

Two of the 'support' systems had waiting lists; George and his wife had never reached the top of either list. The other two provided sporadic and sometimes unreliable assistance. Even permanent institutionalisation involved a nine-month waiting list—or three months if you had the funds to pay for it privately. But George wasn't ready to put his wife in an institution.

He acquired most of his support skills from staff in the hospital while her infections were being treated. Physiotherapy for the chest and limbs; how to feed effectively; how to prevent pressure areas; and how to detect the infections before they took her life. At sixty-eight, George's own life had come to a halt. He had been confined to his house almost twenty-four hours a day for the last three years, helped by some community-based care in the home for the last six months. He found it increasingly difficult to lift Lorraine in and out of the bath, to change her nappies and to dress her. He was also very lonely. Friends and family rarely visited.

I met George during the course of Lorraine's fifth hospital admission. The intravenous fluids and antibiotics were not enough to stabilise her. She was the subject of an urgent call on the wards for low blood pressure.

When I arrived on the general ward to assess her suitability for admission to the ICU, George was distraught and the overworked nurses on the general wards were run off their feet. I agreed to admit her to the ICU with limitations to treatment. We were to continue the antibiotics and fluids but not to put her on life support machines, nor to give her drugs to support her blood pressure.

In the relatives' room I explained to George that severe dementia was a fatal condition and his wife was coming to the end of her life. He was shocked. 'Nobody told me that!' I tried to explain how the fragmentation of medicine and healthcare delivery can often give mixed messages—or, in this case, almost no messages.

I followed up the conversation the next day with another meeting. This time George was accompanied by his two sons and daughter. I explained that their mother's condition was terminal. We would cease the monitoring and do no more investigations; we would forget about the rigid visiting times and number of visitors allowed at any one time and attend to Lorraine's comfort and theirs.

Lorraine died two hours after we talked, by which time George had gone home to catch up on some much-needed sleep. I asked the nurse to ring George and tell him his wife had suddenly deteriorated but not that she had died. This is the normal procedure after someone has died. Maybe it's something to do with the impersonal nature of the phone. The police usually also personally deliver the news of a death rather than over the phone.

The ward round was finished and I was standing by my car, about to leave the hospital, when I saw George arrive. He was clearly anxious, wondering, I supposed, how she could have deteriorated even further than the state she was in before he had left. For a moment I considered following him back up to the ICU. To be there. To explain and share. No, I decided finally. I had said all that was necessary. George and his family now needed to grieve in their own way.

8
Denise's manifesto

I married late in life—to Bobbi Ballas, an American woman who had been living in Australia for over forty years. There is little written about falling in love late in life. One has an image of politeness, friendship mixed with some quaintness, sharing interests associated with the aged such as gardening, lawn bowls, reading and other things people do in the stereotypical version of retirement. There doesn't seem to be much written about passion, excitement and sharing the new and previously unknown. But a different world opened up for me after meeting Bobbi. A bonus was sharing our families. We had both had similar childhood family experiences which, like many, were not quite functional. This seemed to have resulted in siblings from both families who could instantly relate to each other; the same warmth, generosity, black humour and fierce loyalty. A love of each other's families added another dimension to our relationship.

By the time I met Bobbi, her elder sister Denise had quite advanced motor neurone disease; a cruel relentless disease, causing muscle wasting until you become totally paralysed, if you live that long. It also affects the muscles controlling swallowing so that the lungs are not protected from aspirating food and fluid. Usually, as a final event, the diaphragm becomes paralysed so that breathing becomes impossible. In one way, the cruellest part is that the mind is intact during the whole disease progression as you gradually choke and fail to breathe.

I was fortunate to meet Denise when she still had enough muscle function to get around with the assistance of walking sticks. Gradually, she became confined to a wheelchair and then lost most of her upper limb function, leaving her with just enough function in one hand to operate the buttons on her wheelchair. Her husband Paul, a hero if ever there was one, spent his life helping Denise adjust to the gradual onset of infirmity. He did the cooking and housework as well as buying and modifying a car to take her wheelchair. He had to wash and dress her and lift her in and out of beds and wheelchairs. This was difficult for both of them as they had been proud, independent and hard-working people.

On returning to Australia after one visit, I offered to go back to the United States to assist them if they needed to plan Denise's end-of-life care. They had focused on the day-to-day challenges of adapting to whatever changes were required to enable survival. They weren't yet ready to plan for the end.

I had been back in Australia for about four months when I was contacted by Paul, asking me if I could come over to Oregon to help them to navigate Denise's final few months.

I was familiar with patients dying in intensive care units as a result of withdrawal of active management or by not escalating treatment. I had learnt from colleagues, as well as patients and their carers, how to frame discussions around death and dying in an honest and, I hope, compassionate way. However, this was different to planning end of life in the community, with close friends and relatives. Before leaving Australia

I also took advice from a palliative care physician. She emphasised trying to differentiate between fighting for extra life and fighting for other things you value, and to ask Denise what things would be most important to her if time grew short. I should try to understand what factors would cause anxiety, such as money, pain, shortness of breath, embarrassment and Paul's welfare during the process of dying. I should ask questions like: Do you understand the prognosis and what it means for how you want to live? What are your major concerns? Who do you want to make decisions when you can't? How do you want to spend your time? What trade-offs would you accept?

In Denise's case, I believed my role was to listen to what her wishes were and provide information about the disease process so that her own and Paul's wishes were consistent with the reality of the probable clinical course. However, as it was the United States, not Australia, I didn't understand what was available and at what cost. I was acutely aware that many Americans become bankrupt as a result of inappropriate treatment in the terminal stages of their illness. However, I thought we would come to that later, after establishing the general outline of Denise's choices.

Paul and Denise wanted to get down to business soon after I arrived. We agreed to call their plan 'Denise's manifesto'. Issues and scenarios were discussed backwards and forwards. After two days we had completed the manifesto, ready for the meeting with Denise's family practitioner the following day.

DENISE'S MANIFESTO

- Denise believes she hasn't got much longer to live.
- Denise wants to die at home.
- Over the next few months Denise would like to spend as much time as possible in her own home.
- If convenient, she would like visits from her family, bearing in mind that she can tire easily.
- Both Paul and Denise would like to keep the family informed of Denise's condition by email. Her daughter, Julie, would compose the email updates, which would be approved by Paul and Denise and then sent to all family members at the same time.
- Denise would like relief from suffering such as itching, pain, shortness of breath and excessive anxiety.

- Where possible, Denise would like to remain conscious even if she is drowsy as a result of drugs to relieve suffering.
- Denise would like to participate in all decisions that relate to her and Paul.
- If Denise loses consciousness, then her wishes will be the responsibility of Paul.
- If death is imminent Denise would like to have close family with her, depending on her degree of exhaustion.
- Denise would like her brother, Kelly, to distribute her ashes in the Salmon River, where they played as children.

Other eventualities

Artificial ventilation

Denise does not want to have a tracheostomy or be put on any sort of breathing machine in a hospital under any circumstances.

Gallstones

It is possible that a large gallstone may obstruct the bile duct causing the same symptoms as she had had previously, i.e. severe pain, possible biliary infection and pancreatitis (inflammation of the pancreas, a gland near the bile duct). In that case, there are two choices: first, treat the pain at home and perhaps the stone will pass; second, Denise could go to an acute hospital to explore further options regarding removing the stone. If surgery would result in relief of pain, then she would like the condition managed in hospital.

Infection

In Denise's case, there were several possible sources of infection, including urinary tract, pneumonia and infection related to the biliary tract.

Denise knows that an infection is a likely way her life will end and that antibiotics may temporarily get on top of the infection but that the underlying cause of the infection will remain, e.g. inability to effectively clear her sputum as her diaphragm weakens.

Denise has decided that she will make the choice about antibiotic use at the time of the infection. For example, while she is relatively healthy at this time, she would probably have the infection treated at home. At some time in the future she may not take any antibiotics.

Feeding tube

While Denise has relatively good use of her swallowing and vocal muscles, as part of the disease process she has had a lot of her independence and ways of relating to the world reduced, especially when it comes to movement. She will always be able to enjoy sight and hearing but she would like the pleasure of taste kept intact. Obviously, it is a matter of trading risks and benefits. Denise will delay the decision to have a feeding tube and plans on leaving the final decision until the last possible moment.

Denise and Paul thought about options such as euthanasia, which is legal in the state of Oregon. We talked about how it might not be necessary, as there are drugs that will relieve the feeling of shortness of breath and pain and they could be self-delivered according to Denise's needs.

The next day, the three of us went to meet Denise's family practitioner. I was introduced as their in-law and also a doctor from Australia. Having a doctor in the family can sometimes help matters, but can also be regarded with suspicion by the treating doctor.

I tried to reassure her by adding that I was an intensive care specialist and was mainly there as a friend and perhaps to translate some of the medical issues into a reality that they could relate to.

Paul read out the manifesto, as Denise tired easily. It was hard to tell exactly, but I thought that the practitioner seemed initially intrigued but soon became a bit bored and impatient.

After Paul had finished, we all looked at her. She said: 'Easy, perfect, this will all be covered under hospice care provided by the Medicare system.'

My immediate reaction was to emphasise that Denise had decided not to be admitted to a hospice. The doctor then explained that the word 'hospice' referred to a bundle of patient-centred treatments, not an institution. The care included daily visits by a palliative care nurse; weekly visits by physiotherapists, occupational therapists and a music therapist—yes, a musician who would visit Denise at home to play the harp for an hour!

There was more. Denise could be admitted to the local hospital while Paul took five days' respite care. There was no limit on the number of respite care options but they could last no more than five days at a time.

The doctor handed us the appropriate forms. Basically, hospice care was available for patients who had an estimated survival time of less than six months. Care could extend beyond six months so long as the patient's condition continued to merit such a medical outlook. Moreover, it was free!

Summary of the hospice care plan

Hospice care was administered through Medicare but funded through Paul and Denise's medical insurance. Once you are on the hospice plan you have to come off it in order to receive active treatment for the terminal disease: this was no real problem for Denise, as there is no specific active treatment for motor neurone disease. Even then, you can go on hospice and come off it as necessary.

The hospice plan includes:
- 24/7 nursing on call.
- 24/7 doctor on call.
- Nursing visits by appointment, unlimited and as required.
- Initial physiotherapy assessment and then follow-up as required.

- Initial occupational therapist assessment and then appointments as required.
- Initial social worker assessment and then appointments as required.
- Chaplain as needed.
- Speech therapist for assessment and follow-up.
- Dietary counselling.
- Possibility of a musician to play in the home.
- Access to a massage in the home.
- Someone to bathe, attend to personal needs and change linen—up to about four hours, twice or three times a week. This would give Paul a chance to do shopping and other chores.
- Trained volunteers to assist with lifting, respite care, shopping, bathing, dressing etc.
- Respite care in a local hospital is possible in order to give the carer a break. This would be for a maximum of five days but for an unlimited number of times. This could be used by Paul in order to attend special out-of-town events, visit family, when he was not well or just when he needed a break.
- Unlimited supply of drugs to address issues such as pain, shortness of breath, anxiety, muscle spasm

or any unpleasant symptoms related to Denise's condition. The drugs would be picked up from the pharmacy and delivered. The nurses would work with Paul and Denise to determine doses, frequencies etc. The drugs would be supplied at minimum or no cost.

- Appropriate equipment would also be supplied at no cost, including a wheelchair, walkers and lifters as well as bandages, catheters and so on.

Denise's family doctor would direct all care but worked with a relatively autonomous team of nurses, volunteers and other health professionals. No more than two palliative care nurses would be assigned to Denise's case in order to provide continuity, and they would arrange their leave accordingly. The nurses were also available at all times by phone for urgent calls. The team designated to care for Denise would meet every fortnight to discuss and plan for the next two weeks. Denise's team also included pharmacists, counsellors, home health aides and volunteers. The system is built around the patient's needs. Generally, treatment is not diagnostic or curative, unless the treatment is seen to improve quality of life.

Denise signed up. Becky, the palliative care nurse, arrived the following day. She instantly won the trust of Denise and Paul. She was honest, straightforward, funny and compassionate; she didn't dodge any questions and even proposed a few of her own insights and suggestions for the journey they were about to undertake together.

This was a Rolls-Royce service, equivalent to the patient-centred community health systems of Scandinavian countries. But it is to be found in America, the home of one of the most profit-driven and inefficient health services in the world.

Interestingly, most Americans are only referred to hospice care at the very end-stage of their disease. Many physicians are apparently unduly optimistic about the value of conventional active medical management. One-third of hospice patients die within seven days of admission. The reasons for the reluctance to engage such a service are complex. Patients, their carers and their physicians may see it as giving up. Perhaps reimbursements to primary physicians may be difficult to access. Costs are a complicating issue in the United States and as there are many agencies involved, reimbursement to doctors may be inadequate or delayed. Reluctance to use hospice care by patients and physicians alike may be related to the stigma associated with the term; instead of emphasising that different care is required in this phase of the illness, there is a feeling that it means 'there is nothing left to do'.

How did the concept of hospice care come about? Compassion? A commitment to equal access and a standard of care for all? Perhaps that's what it indirectly achieved but it was established because it was the most efficient cost model. Medicare patients who receive hospice care must waive other medical benefits that could prolong life.

The model doesn't include expensive chemotherapy, radiotherapy and support in an ICU for patients in the last six months of life, where treatment and cures were no longer considered appropriate options. In other words, under the hospice plan, aiming to prolong life in the face of terminal illness was not an option. Interestingly, in a famous research trial of terminally ill patients who were offered full active treatment or active treatment plus hospice care, the latter group lived longer and cost less to treat. Many patients in the trial sensed that the active treatment wasn't helping and they wanted a more honest and supportive management.

In Denise's case there was neither cure nor benefit from other measures such as chemotherapy, surgery or radiotherapy. And she was adamant that she did not want to spend her last days with a tracheostomy on a ventilator.

⌣

On the night before I returned to Australia Denise, Paul and I had a meal with Denise's siblings. After dinner, I read out Denise's manifesto and explained how her wishes were to be accommodated by the hospice system. We then discussed their roles in handling her ashes and where they were to be scattered as well as other details which only an organised elder sister could have thought of. A few toasts and a bit more wine later, and I concluded one of the most memorable and satisfying few days I've ever experienced in my life.

Denise survived another nine months, utilising all the services available to her at one time or another, apart from the harpist. While her death was incredibly sad for all of us, we were glad she was able to spend her remaining months in full knowledge of what was to come, cared for by professionals working in a model that should be available to all of us. She died with dignity and free of pain.

9
Intensive care
sans frontières

Many lessons were learnt as the specialty of intensive care developed. Ventilator settings appropriate for normal lungs were found to result in the destruction of frailer lungs. Smaller breaths, consistent with the reduced amount of normal lung, are now routinely delivered. Spontaneous breathing is encouraged and ventilators have been developed which sense the patient's respiration and deliver the exact amount of breath at the most appropriate pressures. Continuous haemodialysis is available for patients with kidney failure. Powerful drugs to support the heart and circulation are given through special cannulae inserted near the heart. Complex machinery such as extracorporeal membrane oxygenation (ECMO) and intra-aortic balloon pump (IABP) can also be used to support the circulation. There are also the generic requirements of caring for all seriously ill patients, such as feeding, the prevention of deep venous thrombosis, sedation and pain relief.

As the specialty developed, more drugs and interventions enabled us to support more of the body's functions until the illness abated. It is interesting to consider the minimum functions that the body needs for survival in the intensive care unit. In theory, limbs are not needed while you are seriously ill, and the kidneys, the gastrointestinal tract, the heart and lungs can all be replaced by machines, leaving only the liver and brain—perhaps the next challenge?

The development of the specialty almost certainly had to occur within four walls, in a specially designed part of the hospital. The ICU not only had to accommodate the machines, monitors and other equipment surrounding patients, but it also facilitated the development of the role of specialist doctors and nurses. The specialty could develop and mature, gradually establishing its legitimacy and recognition by colleagues.

Over time it was noted that intensive care could contribute to the prolongation of life. It is rare for patients to suddenly and unexpectedly die in an intensive care unit. Over 90 per cent of deaths are orchestrated and expected as a result of either withdrawing or withholding active management, whereas in the general ward areas of a hospital there remained a high incidence of potentially preventable deaths and serious adverse events. The majority of potentially preventable deaths and cardiac arrests in acute hospitals are preceded by a long period of documented deterioration in the patient's condition.

There are many reasons for this discrepancy in care. Patients in an ICU are intensely monitored and are managed by a high staffing level of highly skilled doctors and nurses. The situation of patient safety on the general wards of acute hospitals is exacerbated by the changing nature of the hospital population. Patients are now older, with a greater number of chronic illnesses, and are having more complex and potentially dangerous procedures. As a result, staff from intensive care now play a role across the whole hospital in the form of rapid response systems in many countries around the world.

These systems all have two elements in common. First, at-risk patients are *identified* by observing abnormal vital signs, such as the blood pressure, level of consciousness, respiratory rate and pulse rate. An important additional criterion is 'concern'. For the first time nursing staff are empowered and encouraged to call for urgent assistance if they are concerned for the patient's welfare. Once identified, the second element is a *rapid response* by staff whose level of expertise matches the patient's need.

It's not rocket science. Instead of waiting until the patient dies, has a cardiac arrest or another serious event, at-risk patients are identified by well-recognised and universally collected patient information and rapidly responded to by staff with relevant skills and experience. It bypasses the usual hierarchies that have historically existed in hospitals for decades and designs the system around patient needs.

As with the early days of intensive care, there was initial resistance to treating the seriously ill in a different way. Prior to the establishment of ICUs there was the feeling by medical specialists in acute hospitals that the care they provided in the general wards was optimal. There were no alternatives. Many of us remember trying to establish an intensive care unit, a small area in a hospital, where patients could be kept alive in ways not possible in the general wards. The admitting specialist often resisted relinquishing care to other specialists, and this was complicated by political, territorial and even financial issues. There was the common argument that all we needed to do was train the admitting team better and we wouldn't need these expensive ICUs. However, slowly, caring for the seriously ill in an intensive care unit became an accepted and unquestioned practice.

Just as important as saving lives and preventing serious complications, the concept of rapid response systems uncovered a major issue in acute hospitals wherever they were implemented. The systems were initially designed to detect seriously ill and deteriorating patients early. A rapid response would then hopefully prevent death and serious complications. What had not been thought through was that it would also detect patients who were naturally and predictably dying. It is obvious in retrospect. It is impossible to die or have a cardiac arrest, whether it is in a person with every hope of recovering or in someone who is naturally coming to the end of their life, without being recognised at some point in their deterioration by the rapid response system.

But surely there would not be many of these patients? A system that would significantly reduce mortality was striking enough, but just as important was the fact that the system had uncovered the sobering fact that about one-third of all rapid response calls in acute hospitals were for patients at the end of life. In other words, dying patients in acute hospitals were not being recognised until they were so seriously ill as to require an urgent call from staff whose role was to save lives, not diagnose dying. The figures are staggering. A teaching hospital may have at least six of these calls each day, meaning about two patients each day or 700 patients each year are not recognised as being at the end of life until they are close to death.

In other words, an acute hospital may be ideal if you have an illness amenable to a proven treatment, but if you are an elderly frail person with little in the way of reversibility of your clinical conditions, you will not be recognised as such. This is a serious failing of the clinicians working in hospitals. Perhaps it is a lack of appropriate training or maybe a reluctance to discuss such issues because it implies failure on their behalf. Or perhaps they simply cannot recognise patients at the end of life and determine when discussions need to occur with the patients and their carers and different goals of care need to be considered.

There is an obvious and pressing need to address this issue. Research around recognising people at the end of life is urgently needed. However, there is also an urgent need to build a system around the needs of patients similar to the rapid response system.

This would require more than modifying the behaviour of existing players in hospitals but establishing an organisational system for responding to patients rapidly and with staff who have appropriate expertise and skills. These would include the ability to conduct honest discussions with patients and their carers about their prognosis and what their wishes are in view of their outlook. Important issues such as symptomatic treatment and the place of care and support for them and their carers would also need to be discussed.

In the meantime, especially for the elderly frail, beware of acute hospitals, as they may not have much to offer you in terms of recognising that you are near the end of your life or listening to what your wishes may be. Even more sobering, they might not have any insight into these shortcomings.

10
Diagnostic dilemmas

I was dealing with two angry colleagues who were arguing about who 'owned' Madeleine, the eighty-five-year-old woman in bed 4. Both specialists had heavy clinical workloads and were manoeuvring to avoid yet another admission. Ironically, the patient was an elderly woman for whom little more could be done in terms of curative treatment. Maybe that was the reason why neither wanted the patient admitted under them.

Madeleine came in with shortness of breath on the back of a long history of smoking. She had been in hospital six times over the last few months, each time for shortness of breath related to her smoking.

Unfortunately, you can't smoke as much as she had for over sixty years without also destroying other organs, including the heart. Accordingly, Madeleine also had some heart failure, contributing to the shortness of breath. The respiratory physician responsible for the lung damage as a result of smoking was heatedly pointing out that her chest X-ray had changes consistent with heart failure. The cardiologist acknowledged that but said the main reason for the shortness of breath was the underlying damage caused by the smoking. Possession is everything in this game and the patient had already been admitted under the respiratory representative. He was stuck with her. This occurs every day. It drives the emergency doctors to despair, as it is left to them to negotiate the conflict.

Diseases in conventional medicine are divided into *acute* and *chronic*. *Acute* refers to the rapidity of onset, not the severity of the disease. *Chronic* refers to the underlying and usually permanent state of health. An example is the acute onset of a urinary tract infection in an elderly frail person who has multiple chronic problems, such as heart failure, dementia and chronic kidney disease. The acute problem is easily fixed: antibiotics and maybe intravenous fluid. However, the real problem, the major determinant of the patient's prognosis, is the underlying chronic health status.

The seventeenth-century English physician Thomas Sydenham described acute diseases as those when God is the author and chronic as those that originate in ourselves. Medicine concentrates on the acute disease. It is what doctors are trained to treat. The acute diagnosis is how the hospital classifies the admission; it is the basis for financial reimbursement; it is the source of most of the data on which we plan our health systems. This ignores the fact that, in the case of the urinary tract infection in the elderly, the chronic health status is not only the underlying reason for the acute disease but will ultimately determine the outcome.

Unfortunately, many elderly frail people are usually admitted to acute hospitals for management of their so-called acute condition. In an age of medical specialisation, and because most elderly admissions have multiple problems, a patient could be admitted under any of four or five medical subspecialists. It is a largely random process and may vary at every admission.

Like most elderly patients being admitted to hospital, Madeleine had a host of age-related conditions, or co-morbidities, that did not lend themselves to the concept of a single diagnosis. She also had diabetes, high blood pressure and chronic renal failure. Other age-related chronic health problems include coronary heart disease, elevated cholesterol, gastro-oesophageal regurgitation syndrome, osteoarthritis, previous stroke, heart failure, peripheral vascular disease and chronic respiratory problems. They are such a common feature of the patients admitted to our intensive care unit that we are considering having a stamp made so all we have to do is tick those that are present. The conditions all have medical labels but are almost invariably only found as one ages. Unfortunately, these underlying conditions do not lend themselves well to treatment by conventional medicine. Our hospitals increasingly contain these elderly frail patients. However, very few doctors honestly explain the impact of ageing and that, despite the miracles of modern medicine, little can be done in terms of a cure. But a lot could be done in terms of honest discussion about the patient's chronic health status and its probable course.

The concept of a diagnosis is integral to the teaching and practice of medicine. We 'reach' or 'make' a diagnosis. 'What is wrong with me, Doctor?' has to be unravelled by finding a diagnosis. The assumption is that there is a single diagnosis. Medical practice is based on the concept of the diagnosis. Getting to the bottom of a patient's problem is one of the prime goals of clinical practice. It is based on taking a history from the patient; performing a physical examination; establishing differential diagnoses; performing investigations; and, bingo, there it is—the diagnosis!

Diseases are classified by the World Health Organization using the International Classification of Diseases (ICD). It is used in over 110 countries, in forty-two languages, for clinical and epidemiological purposes as well as for health management, reimbursement and resource allocation. The ICD codes for diseases, signs and symptoms, abnormal findings, complaints, social circumstances and external causes of injury and disease, allowing for more than 14,400 different codes and up to 16,000 codes when optional sub-classifications are added.

In an attempt to make sense of diagnoses, the concept of diagnosis-related groups (DRGs) was introduced by the Yale School of Management in the early 1980s. The fact that it was developed by a School of Management should have rung alarm bells. It was developed to identify 'products' that hospitals provide. A specific diagnosis was assigned a certain reimbursement. If you managed the diagnostic problem quickly and without complications you would make a profit. If not, you didn't. It was a financial tool, not a medical one, constructed around reducing health care to costs. Nevertheless, the system is used universally.

In theory, it made sense. If you were having a simple procedure, such as the removal of your gall bladder, there was a specific diagnostic label: cholecystectomy. If the operation went well, you were reimbursed a certain amount. If there were complications which increased hospital stay, it was your fault and you bore the cost.

It's not surprising that a whole industry has developed, aimed at 'gaming' the system. A diagnostic system built on such flexible interpretations means the accountants can designate the most financially advantageous label. Hospitals with the most imaginative accountants are seen as the better hospitals. For example, savvy hospitals with the right accountants can improve their mortality from pneumonia by recoding such deaths under other labels such as 'respiratory failure' or 'sepsis'. Similarly, certain labels attracting less funding are recoded under high reimbursement codes. This has nothing to do with the delivery of good health care.

Madeleine didn't fit this accountancy-based construct and neither do most of the elderly patients who are currently admitted to our hospitals. The population of patients in the developed world has changed and the concept of a single diagnosis is less relevant. People are now living longer and have an increasing number of chronic age-related conditions. No matter how the ICD and DRG systems have modified their codes, the name or number or even collections of names and numbers do not accurately define the clinical state of the patient. The list of 'diseases' or 'diagnoses' has now increased to over many tens of thousands, as we understand more about pathophysiology and with access to more complex ways of investigating patients. I can imagine that 200 years ago people died of a limited number of conditions such as cholera, typhus, tuberculosis. pneumonia, trauma, septicaemia and issues related to childbirth. Today, in developing countries, young people also die as a result of a single condition such as tuberculosis, malaria, HIV-related diseases and trauma.

But as our understanding of medicine increases, and with the powerful imaging and sophisticated tests that we have today, new conditions are found almost daily.

However, it is not only about the miracles of modern medicine and making the rare diagnosis. Rather, it is about exploring the changing nature of the patient population; how this relates to the concept of the diagnosis; how that concept is changing; as well as the implications of such change. In particular, we need to explore the shortcomings of rigid diagnostic codes in describing the normal processes of ageing and dying. The specialty of renal medicine, for example, is considering expanding its boundaries by labelling the normal age-related deterioration of their organ, the kidney, as chronic kidney disease. This will mean that almost half of people over the age of seventy-five years of age will have this 'disease'.

Despite radical changes in the population of hospital patients, acute hospitals still function in much the same way as they have for over fifty years. Emergency departments remain an appendage to the core business of the hospital. Up until about the 1960s, they used to be places for patients who could not afford private health care in their own home or in the doctor's rooms.

As acute hospitals became the flagships of health care, the role of community-based care changed. Hospitals became places where the technology and medical expertise was concentrated. Society was aware of this and, as such, patients gravitated to the emergency departments of acute hospitals. As a result, emergency department presentations are increasing dramatically, especially in patients over the age of eighty-five.

Nowadays, people don't get sick and die within days and weeks. They become old and, in the process, gradually collect conditions relating to wearing out as a result of ageing. They are fighting a losing battle. It is common for the elderly to be increasingly admitted to hospital in the last few months of their lives. The accountants who increasingly influence the way we practise medicine still believe in the concept that a patient is admitted with a single diagnosis; the problem is fixed and they are sent home. Therefore, for the patient to be readmitted means the problem wasn't solved. The single diagnosis wasn't treated appropriately and the patient returned to the hospital as a readmission. There are whole industries dedicated to fixing the problem of hospital readmissions. Hospitals can be scrutinised for having a higher than expected readmission rate.

The inference is that the hospital has done something wrong and needs to be punished. The readmission may be a sign that the hospital failed to resolve the patient's problem adequately. This in turn could be related to the patient being discharged too early, as delayed discharge also incurs financial punishment. However, the elderly are increasingly admitted to acute hospitals as ageing is irreversible and the medical problems associated with ageing become worse, requiring repeated admissions. This is just the way the medicalisation of dying has distorted our health system. As a result, hospitals are financially punished for treating a certain population of patients not on the quality of the service they provide, but for operating in a society which pretends that diseases as a result of ageing are always treatable. They are also punished for the failure of society to be honest about what medicine can and, more importantly, can't do. They are punished for the failure of society to provide and fund more appropriate end-of-life care for our elderly.

Rightly or wrongly many of these age-related conditions have been medicalised. Doctors make negligible or no contributions to the health of elderly frail patients. But it doesn't stop them incrementally prescribing one drug after another to a person who is on an inevitable decline. And sometimes doctors cause pain and suffering by subjecting elderly patients to unnecessary operations and even condemning them to spend their last few days on machines in an intensive care unit.

Together with the increase in medical specialisation, a perverse situation has developed. The ageing individual with multiple issues or diagnoses has their conditions artificially divided up among single-organ specialists: experts who attempt to fine-tune their own organ with little regard to the overall picture. These are the 'sick elderly' who comprise the majority of patients now admitted to acute hospitals. Ironically they require 'sick elderly' care that in most cases is not available in acute hospitals. Instead of simply more tablets and interventions, the care should perhaps be designed around the patient's functionality and their wishes. Many would prefer to be treated in their own home or a community-based facility, rather than spending the end of their lives in hospital.

Even though the elderly frail rarely fit into a single diagnostic category, 'making the diagnosis' is still at the heart of medicine. Finding the rare diagnosis is the subject of the weekly Case Records of the Massachusetts General Hospital Grand Rounds in the *New England Journal of Medicine*. Getting the right diagnosis in this weekly puzzle is like cracking the *Times* crossword. The television series *House* used to be one of the most popular shows on television. Its star was an eccentric and often abrupt doctor with a limp and a personality disorder. But he is the stuff of legends because he unravelled the case and came up with the correct and invariably rare diagnosis.

There is nothing wrong with cracking the rare diagnosis but the main focus of medicine is caring for patients. Some of them may be among the grateful few that have a rare disorder but the majority of patients will have a complex interaction of chronic medical and social issues that require equally complex solutions.

I used to think that general physicians such as the acute care physician or hospitalists might offer the balance needed to manage these patients. However, they too have usually learnt their medicine in the conventional way and are focused on diagnoses and cure. Similarly, geriatricians seem to be more like general physicians of the aged and many are reluctant to practise outside the boundaries of conventional medicine. There are the exceptions who believe that the traditional approach of modern medicine does not work well for old people. Perhaps the anecdotes of our medical colleagues, when considering stories about our own dying relatives, may change the obsession with conventional medical practice to one of more compassionate and patient-focused care. Unfortunately, it is often easier and more financially rewarding to perform expensive diagnostic tasks and interventions than to spend time explaining, addressing symptoms, considering the social circumstances and being honest with patients and their carers.

If one wants to define the indistinct zone of chronic illness and age-related deterioration we could look at the sum of the individual medical terms and give it a collective meaning which reflects the patient's condition. This does not mean that we neglect the medical conditions which may respond well to conventional medicine but that we acknowledge to ourselves and our patients that people become frailer as they age and we will do everything to help them to adjust and manage the unpleasant symptoms associated with ageing.

'Old age' or 'frailty' are not, as yet, acceptable diagnoses. Unfortunately, neither is 'dying'. It is sobering to ponder on the fact that acute hospitals, with all their resources and well-trained clinicians, often do not recognise patients who are at the end of life. Appropriate management of dying is lost in the incremental management of the myriad of ICD diagnostic codes.

Predicting the exact time of death is difficult, but that does not mean that it should never be discussed openly with patients and their carers. Palliative care has been useful in the management of end-stage cancer. The specialty is increasingly becoming involved in other conditions, such as heart failure. However, even palliative care is a diagnosis-based specialty and has yet to engage on a wide scale with people who are just naturally coming to the end of their life as a result of ageing and increasing frailty. Palliative care teams could potentially contribute greatly to the care of those people with honest explanations, simple symptom control and appropriate support.

There are many other implications to the way diagnoses are currently defined and classified. It is obligatory in our history taking that we ask about family illness, including the cause of death of a patient's parents and even grandparents. It's easy when they died of a heart attack at the age of forty with no obvious preceding illnesses. But what do patients say when their parents or grandparents gradually became frailer and died at the age of eighty-five? More than likely they will tell you of what was written on the death certificate or repeat what the doctor in the hospital said. Death certificates are notoriously inaccurate However, according to the certificate, people have to die of specific diagnostic causes and this needs to be stated on the death certificate. It has been said that the inaccuracy of death certificates may be due to factors such as laziness or the lack of knowledge and training of junior doctors, who are usually the ones given the task of signing the form. However, as most of us know when filling out a death certificate, it is often guesswork. In many patients it appears as if everything has just come to a halt. The person had just faded away due to multiple and predictable organ failures as a result of old age. This does not lend itself to rigid and medically based diagnoses. The coding follows international guidelines and is subject to strict statistical modelling. But if the underlying data is inaccurate, it is a case of 'rubbish in, rubbish out'.

Unfortunately, our health system and services are built around such erroneous data. For example, we may hear that the most common killer in our community is cardiovascular disease. The corollary is that we must devote more resources to this problem. The conclusion overlooks the randomness and inaccuracy associated with what is on the death certificate as well as the fact that much of the clinical state of the elderly is not amenable to preventable or curative medicine. And, of course, you die when your heart stops beating, no matter what else contributed to your demise. So it's often easy to state that you died a cardiovascular death.

However, many patients have just become old and things have worn out. It seems illogical to assign a strict diagnostic code or even series of names to this terminal condition rather than to use terms such as 'old age' or frailty. The patient possibly just faded away with decreasing mobility, weight loss, tiredness and lack of will to keep going. Lay people, when asked how their relative died, are unlikely to list all the co-morbidities. And even if they could provide the clinician with the list, does that mean the person

DIAGNOSTIC DILEMMAS

giving the family medical history will be more or less likely to accumulate the same list? Possibly, but not when the list simply represents the normal ageing process which they, like their deceased relatives, will undergo: a gradually decreasing resistance to infection or perhaps the inevitable decrease in muscle bulk and strength that led to the fall that 'killed' them.

Albert, the eighty-two-year-old man in bed 9, had a cardiac arrest caused by a lack of oxygen as a result of being a long-term smoker. Like Madeleine, he also had heart problems with narrowing of his coronary arteries. He may have had a critical drop in the oxygen levels needed to sustain his heart, causing it to fibrillate, resulting in a cardiac arrest. The low oxygen levels had been exacerbated by aspirating saliva and food into his lungs as a result of increasing dementia. Perhaps this was on the background of prostate cancer which had caused increasing immobility and decreased immunity, resulting in pneumonia which added to the hypoxia which caused his heart to finally stop. He died after three days. What am I going to write as the cause of death on his certificate? It's hard to separate all of the interacting factors and give one as the major cause. We used to be able to write death from 'old age' once. This would reflect the reality that old age is not, unlike cardiovascular disease, a public health issue to be prevented. It may also inform our society that death is inevitable; that the claims of modern medicine are often unrealistic and exaggerated.

In the specialty of intensive care, we use the term 'multi-organ failure'. It usually refers to an acute insult such as infection or trauma causing many organs to malfunction. However, the term could be accurately applied to the elderly with organs that are all becoming dysfunctional and failing.

We have certainly made great advances in the improvement of so-called chronic diseases in the elderly. There is no doubt that we are living longer. We have made inroads into the management of strokes, heart attacks and diabetes. But we are left with elderly people with an increasing list of age-related conditions for which modern medicine with all its miracles is making little impact. The great advances in medicine have been classified under curative and preventative medicine. We are now moving into a different area which is not obsessed with mindlessly prolonging life but which is about identifying the limits of modern medicine, being honest with people and devoting resources to supporting people in more imaginative and innovative ways as they age and begin dying.

The single acute diagnosis is often a random and inaccurate description of why the patient needs hospitalisation. They need to be hospitalised because they are too ill to be cared for in the community and because their carers, often elderly themselves, cannot provide the physically taxing attention required for their care. Many of these patients are terminally ill in the last few days or weeks of their life. The diagnostic code, even modified by co-morbidities, does not describe their clinical state.

However, patients want to know what is wrong with them. We probably need a new language in which to engage medical knowledge with the patient's problem. In the case of the elderly frail, there is the complexity associated with the physiological nature of ageing and deteriorating organ function. All of our organs deteriorate with age. This information could be translated into a general description of ageing using examples, so that the patient understands that these things may not as yet add up to a diagnosis but more a condition of health that will get worse at rates that we're not too sure about. Then one would need to explain the nature of the so-called co-morbidities, such as high blood pressure, coronary artery disease and osteoarthritis, along with an explanation about how these age-related conditions might be amenable to symptomatic treatment or therapy aimed at modifying the course of the disease. Doctors could increasingly use this sort of language rather than talking in terms of a diagnosis. During discussions, a good doctor would never avoid uncertainty or answers such as 'I'm not too sure' or 'I don't know'.

It has always been tempting for doctors to resort to the certainty of the current state of knowledge rather than drifting into acknowledging uncertainty. In the case of an aged frail person we may not know exactly how long they have to live but we do know, depending on certain health and functional factors, that it may be a matter of months or perhaps a year or two. Patients and their carers have a right to know this too.

Another approach could be to bundle all the age-related problems that impact on our health and consider them in terms of how they impact on our lives. The accumulated dysfunctions could be expressed in ways that are important to patients, such as reduced mobility, increasing pain, a lower cognitive ability and less independence. These core dimensions are common to many ageing patients, as well as being of great significance to them—more significant than rigid medical diagnoses. We should also recognise that the rigidly defined medical diagnosis could change with time. Heart failure may be mild with few symptoms at one stage of the patient's life, becoming more severe with time and ultimately contributing to severe functional disability. Moving away from rigid diagnostic categories may also result in more personalised care for patients based on what is troubling them most.

Perhaps we should consider defining what an appropriate admission to hospital is? An inappropriate admission would be where the resources of a modern acute hospital does not match the level of the patient's illness or, to put it another way, where the hospital's resources provide no or little improvement in the patient's medical condition, or where indeed the admission may result in an adverse patient outcome.

Moreover, coding diagnoses and reasons for dying may give an erroneous impression of the health challenges we are facing. The names and numbers may not reflect the fact that the patient is simply and predictably dying and where there are no public health issues requiring a redirection of funding to prevent the unpreventable. Modern medicine incrementally operating at the edges of the elderly frail may just be a series of cruel and futile assaults.

The question, 'What is wrong with me, Doctor?' is important to people and requires a careful and honest explanation.

11
Frailty

As our elderly population increases we are developing greater rates of age-related medical conditions. Conditions associated with a normal deterioration in organs such as the heart, lungs, liver, kidney and brain. They are often given medical labels such as coronary artery disease, osteoarthritis, dementia, type 2 diabetes and hypertension. The onset and severity are determined by genes and influenced by environmental factors such as diet, exercise and smoking. Moreover, as we age, there is an increasing chance that cells will miscode, sometimes causing cancers as a result of the normally vigilant immune system failing to do its job effectively. Nor does the ageing body deal with microbes as effectively as it once did.

The sum of all these normal age-related conditions does not, as yet, have a name nor a number. They are usually catalogued under medical conditions and divided up among the various medical specialists, according to which organ is involved. And so, incrementally, you are placed on an increasing number of tablets in order to halt the progress or to 'cure' the 'conditions'. Because of the inevitable and chronic nature of ageing, this approach has limitations. Our society and patients are often not told explicitly about ageing and where we are going with the increasing number of medications and, sometimes, more invasive interventions and operations.

Eventually, the sum of the conditions makes the person vulnerable to relatively minor events such as an infection or fall. Then we focus on this sudden condition, often disregarding the underlying big picture. The sum of the deterioration hasn't, as yet, been assigned a label. As a result, doctors focus on the individual medical problems and not on the person.

Age-related terms such as 'co-morbidities' and 'multiple chronic conditions' are often used interchangeably.

They may have different meanings but ageing is an underlying feature for all of them.

There is some light at the end of the tunnel. Of all the terms used to try to nail ageing with a bit more accuracy, the term 'frailty' is gaining some traction. The end stage of ageing makes people look frail. Frailty is also a good way of describing the increased likelihood of them not being able to resist infection, or to develop cancer or to fall over.

Frailty begins with features such as not being able to undertake exercise as much as before, then an obvious slowing down and being unable to attend to normal activities such as bathing and housework, then being totally dependent on others, and finally being bed-bound and terminally ill.

The term frailty is potentially important as it gets us away from cures. It means that we can talk about ageing in more honest ways, and it also means that we can discuss with more certainty the fact that frail people, when exposed to an injury or infection, have an increased risk of becoming more disabled and even dying. If people were able to define their progressive frailty and the associated prognosis, they may be able to express their wishes about possible active treatment more accurately. They may not even want to annoy or disappoint the hospitals' accountants, depending on whether it is a public or private institution, by coming into expensive hospitals. If given the choice, many may want to be managed in their home or somewhere more appropriate in the community.

There are many frailty measurements and scores based on factors such as gait speed, grip strength and the ability to stand on one leg. Other features of frailty may include: under-nutrition; prolonged confinement to bed; increasing dependence; pressure ulcers; gait disorders; generalised weakness; weight loss; anorexia; increased tendency to fall; dementia; hip fracture; delirium; and confusion. Out of all the indicators of frailty, slow gait is arguably the most accurate. As a result, I find myself observing people who appear to be of my age and comparing my gait speed to theirs. I sometimes try to walk faster, in the hope that it will reduce the rate of my own frailty.

Chronological age is not an accurate determinant of when these disabilities will occur. There is hope that it may not occur early and the hope resides, as usual, in your genetic make-up but also how well you have looked after yourself.

We could use the attributes of frailty to consider important issues, such as how quickly the deterioration may progress, what it will mean in terms of independence and when more assistance is required. This may lead to questions such as: What sort of support will I need? Should I be planning a higher level of care? If so, what is available? And how long do you think I have to live? Frailty measures are much better at predicting your survival into old age than defining your condition in medical terms.

Things are easier when you have a single diagnosis. For example, when someone is diagnosed with cancer, these are the sorts of questions that people ask and, indeed, they have a right to know the answers. As with cancer, the exact progress of the disease, its complications and possible number of months or years left to live, cannot be exactly determined. However, there is enough information about cancer to say that, looking at a large number of similar cases, this is the probable course of your disease and this is the average time you have left.

Frailty and old age is similar to cancer in that your condition may be terminal. You may have, for example, an estimated survival time of about a year.

Every person will progress at a different rate with different degrees of disabilities. However, we can discuss the average time course, the nature of the deterioration and the implications for you in terms of assistance and planning.

Just as important, this would empower people to make choices about how they want to be managed towards the end of their life. For example, they need to be told that, as they become increasingly frail and immobile, they are prone to infections such as pneumonia or urinary tract infections and may need increasing assistance to carry out basic functions of living.

The Canadian Study of Health and Ageing Clinical Frailty Score is one way of defining the concept. It presents the progression from fit to frail in an easy-to-understand way.

1. **Very fit**: Robust, energetic and motivated.
2. **Well**: People who have no active disease symptoms but are less fit than category 1.
3. **Managing well**: People whose 'medical' problems are well controlled but are not regularly active, beyond routine walking.

4. **Vulnerable**: While not dependent on others for daily help, symptoms often limit exercise. A common complaint is 'slowing down' and being tired during the day.

5. **Mildly frail**: More evidently slowing and need help in higher levels of 'activities of daily living', such as transportation, heavy housework and finances. Mild frailty increasingly impairs shopping, walking alone, meal preparation and housework.

6. **Moderately frail**: Require assistance for all outside activities and with housework. They have trouble with stairs and may need increasing assistance with bathing.

7. **Severely frail**: Complete dependence for personal care from either cognitive or physical impairment or a combination of both.

8. **Very severely frail**: Completely dependent, approaching the end of life. Typically they may not recover from even the mildest illness.

9. **Terminally ill**: Applies to people with a life expectancy of less than months.

The presence of frailty in so many in our society has taken us by surprise. We were not ready for it.

Our society does not currently have the appropriate health systems nor the community support for the tsunami of the aged and frail in the next few decades. There is little discussion—no movies, novels, plays or television series which discuss the issue in any depth or with any honesty. Our shared social life has not taken up this challenge.

Many people suffer substantially as a result of the failure to manage easily treatable symptoms and the lack of provision of appropriate environments for managing frailty. Instead we often concentrate on inappropriate and ineffective aggressive medical treatment at the end of life. This is a serious shortcoming in the way we currently manage the elderly frail.

We can predict the likelihood of survival for elderly individuals and groups of patients with some accuracy. However, this does not seem to influence the use of inappropriate and aggressive medical care. Patient safety includes managing the dying and frail safely, not just preventing potentially preventable adverse events. Patterns of care for the frail do not seem to take into account patient and carer choices. In other words, there is little flexible crafting of care available for the frail. Patients and their carers will often be kept in the dark about prognosis and the appropriateness of modern medicine.

Many people in our society will die of one of many forms of cancer. Often this involves a period of time spent in relatively good health soon after a diagnosis has been made, followed by a rapid decline to death. This is not usually the trajectory for dying in the elderly frail. Many people in the developed world will now suffer a slow dwindling of physical and cognitive function as they age. The end is often the result of a relatively minor acute illness such as pneumonia or a urinary tract infection that tests the patient's reserve to its limit and results in death from a cause which would have been a minor inconvenience in a younger person.

Our health system is built around relatively young people developing single-organ problems. Even the management of patients dying of cancer is often delivered by enthusiastic physicians who continue to claim that we can now cure most cancers. Often the patient is put through an ordeal of chemotherapy, radiotherapy and the like in the last few months of life. Much of this treatment is for 'palliation', not cure.

But a different approach is gaining traction. Palliative care teams are being involved early in the treatment of diseases which will eventually be terminal. They work with specialists who deliver what is called 'active treatment'. As the active treatment becomes less effective, the role of the palliative care team providing a broader support role becomes more important. Apart from the obvious benefit of having pain and unpleasant symptoms addressed, there is an honest acknowledgement at an early stage that the disease will eventually be terminal. The contribution of the palliative care team is not seen as the result of failure of real medicine. This is just the beginning in the more appropriate management of cancer and other terminal conditions. However, our health system is not currently constructed in a similar way for the management of the severely frail.

A new system could look something like this:

- Develop more accurate predictors of the onset and progress of frailty and share this information with our society.
- Develop an individualised plan that tracks and stays with that person and their carers across time and in different settings.

- Insist on high standards of symptom prevention and relief, family support and planning ahead.
- Pay sustainable salaries for carers who work in this area and discount from costly interventions, drugs and futile hospital and intensive care admissions.
- Develop support for family and other caregivers, including disability insurance and respite care.
- Concentrate on community-based care according to the patient's condition and their wishes.

What is stopping these developments? Some factors include: unreal expectations of modern medicine; extrapolating the effectiveness of treatments, especially drug therapy, from younger patient populations to the elderly frail at the end of life; politicians afraid to tackle the problem for fear of being labelled 'death merchants'; and lobby groups such as drug companies, equipment manufacturers and medical professionals who have a financial interest in maintaining things as they are.

We are beginning to explore this concept of frailty. We may eventually begin to speak a common language around the medical implications of ageing. However, we need to be wary of a medical profession that often resorts to a 'fight' against diseases. This approach is sometimes appropriate, especially when it results in public health initiatives such as clean water, efficient sanitation and vaccination. However, 'fighting' old age and frailty with drugs and complex interventions is an expensive and largely ineffective exercise. The inference is that frailty may be avoidable or even curable. Apart from giving false hope, it reinforces the current complicity between modern medicine and our society, inferring that all things are treatable or even curable. There is also a danger that frailty will assume a medical life of its own, with specific diagnostic criteria and an assumption that it can be treated. We may gradually lose sight of the inevitability of frailty and be blinded by the prospect of immortality.

12
It is hard to die

Dr Duncan MacDougall of Massachusetts reported in 1907 that the soul weighed three-quarters of an ounce (21 grams) by weighing people immediately before and after death.

It has long been rumoured that Walt Disney intended to have his body frozen soon after his death. According to his daughter Diane, however, Walt never wanted to be frozen. After his death at the age of sixty-five, he was cremated, and his ashes reside at the Forest Lawn Memorial Park in Glendale, California.

Cryogenics, the study of cryonics, is the low-temperature preservation of humans and animals. Ideally, cryonic procedures begin within minutes of the heart stopping in order to prevent deterioration of tissues, so that when the body is warmed at some point in the future, the latest cure for whatever disease afflicted that body in life can be applied. It is particularly important to prevent damage to the brain when circulation ceases, as a lot of time, effort and money would be wasted if, when you were finally unfrozen down the line, your brain no longer worked. We do not know if memory, personality and identity are preserved during the cooling process. In theory, they may be. Depending on your ability to pay, you can either have your head, brain or whole body preserved.

At a conference several years ago I listened in awe as an entrepreneur from Los Angeles talked about his cryopreservation company. As a client is nearing the end of life, a doctor continually monitors the patient, hand on the pulse, watching the breathing. Meanwhile, a truck is waiting around the corner with every life support machine available, manned by technicians who are experts in their operation. When the attending doctor can no longer feel a pulse or detect a breath, he declares the patient dead. Legally, in the western world, a person is dead when a doctor declares them dead.

A quick call is made to the truck driver, who pulls up outside the home. The crew and machines are quickly rolled out of the back of the truck. Like a cardiac arrest team, they descend on the corpse and activate all their machines, such as extracorporeal membrane oxygenation to take over the circulation, artificial ventilation to oxygenate the body and keep the lungs inflated, and intravenous lines in order to deliver life-restoring drugs. As a result, the patient wakes up, and returns to life after being legally dead. Then the process of cryopreservation begins with cooling and cryoprotectants, and the patient gradually dies again. They are cooled to about −196 degrees Celsius, the boiling point of liquid nitrogen. It is thought that crystal formation and other potential causes of cellular destruction are minimised by a process called vitrification.

Then it is a matter of keeping the client frozen until a cure is found for the disease that felled them. A major problem, yet to be addressed, is that old people die of old age. They have lived in an aged body, grey-haired and wrinkled with decreased function in most tissues and organs. They have died as a result of a combination of all these effects. Waking up in this sort of body may not be ideal, even if there is a cure for the final abnormality which resulted in 'death', as the elderly frail rarely die of a single treatable disease. And younger people with a single incurable disease rarely have the funds or perspective to consider cryo-preservation. Cryopreservation's main clients are wealthy elderly people coming to the end of their lives. In time, the DNA could be taken from one of their cells and cleaned up to recreate a younger version or even another version of themselves. But maybe we shouldn't be populating an already overpopulated world with old people near death from another cause or clones of their original selves. Maybe we haven't thought this one through yet.

Aubrey de Grey, on the other hand, wants to stop us ageing in the first place. He used the US$16.5 million he inherited from his mother to fund his SENS Research Foundation aimed at preventing age-related physical and cognitive decline. SENS stands for Strategies for Engineered Negligible Senescence. De Grey aims to succeed where Faust and Dorian Gray failed and without the ominous consequences. He is associated with the Methuselah Mouse Prize, awarded to researchers who can stretch the life span of mice.

He also coined the term 'pro-aging trance', a state of mind designed to put the horror of ageing out of one's mind. *MIT Technology Review* commented that de Grey's proposals were so wrong they were unworthy of learned debate. However, the fear is that no matter how irrational his theories may be, the fear of ageing and dying may trump rational thinking.

Mr Harding was seventy-four and had been in our ICU for about twenty-four hours. He had lived in a small New South Wales country town all his life. He was found in a field by a schoolteacher on his way to work. The teacher commenced CPR and an ambulance took Mr Harding to the local hospital, where the doctor secured intravenous access and gave him drugs to help his circulation. During this time CPR continued. A helicopter was called and the patient was transferred to our hospital. By the time he arrived, he had received CPR for five hours and was still without a pulse of his own. Because his temperature was low, it was thought there was a chance that his brain may not have suffered the almost always inevitable damage after five hours of CPR.

A decision was made to insert an extracorporeal membrane oxygenation (ECMO) machine to take over the function of the heart and lungs. Mr Harding was now in bed 8 on a ventilator as well as having maximum drug therapy to optimise his cardiovascular system. His temperature had returned to normal but he looked for all the world like a corpse. That's because he was. He showed no sign of brain function, and his heart and lungs didn't function without the drugs, ECMO and ventilator. He was legally dead. We were about to stop treatment.

Possibly because they are country folk, his family expressed their gratitude. But they could not understand why we had put him through such an ordeal after he had already died.

Above, I used the case of the cryopreservation company as an example of the perverse lengths to which modern medicine can go in its attempts to preserve life. In light of this, it is interesting to reflect on what we had inflicted on Mr Harding. The Los Angeles patient had been declared dead before having life restored artificially and then frozen. Mr Harding had died and, as a result, cooled down, had 'life' maintained artificially, and was then warmed up and declared dead.

Doctor Elisabeth Kübler-Ross, in her wonderful book *On Death and Dying*, asks: 'Why is it so hard to die well?' She is speaking of the *ars moriendi*, or the art of dying. She suggests that hospitals are not the appropriate place for dying as they are institutions designed for healing, thus equating death with failure. She emphasises 'acceptance' and encourages readers to choose their own way of dying.

In the nineteenth century, much less faith was put in medicine. In fact, there were institutions such as the Edinburgh Association for the Relief of Incurables, which was responsible for building the Royal Edinburgh Hospital for Incurables. At the time there were many such institutions in countries around the world. It is doubtful that we would be so blunt about the shortcomings of medicine today, but all too often we withhold the crucial information that certain people do indeed have incurable conditions. Like Kübler-Ross, I don't think current acute hospitals are the most appropriate place to manage people at the end of life. Obviously, we would need spin doctors to market more appropriate terms when we are speaking of dying. The word 'incurable' would probably not be one of the more acceptable terms.

Perhaps Mrs Mathieson summed up best how difficult it may be to actually die well. She called in during a radio interview I was doing after the publication of my first book, *Vital Signs: Stories from Intensive Care* and related the story of her husband, who had died recently. They'd both made a pact to avoid drastic measures when their time was up. They didn't write their pact down but made their wishes clear to their children.

As they were driving around their country town, Mr Mathieson slumped against Mrs Mathieson, who was driving. She stopped the car and, sure enough, he was dead. She pushed his body away so that he rested against the window. Like many women of her age, she didn't have a mobile phone, but there was a public phone about a hundred metres down the road. She began to drive towards it, then pulled over and thought about what would happen next. If she was to call an ambulance, they would drag him out of the car and start CPR, maybe even bring him back to 'life', take him to hospital and put him on life support machines. No, she decided; that wouldn't do. She resumed driving, and her route took her past the local hospital. And the same scene unfolded in her mind.

Young enthusiastic doctors jumping up and down on her husband, life support, and visions of the nursing home with his blank expression, drooling and being fed like a baby.

Then she heard the sound of bells ringing at the railway crossing just down the road. She accelerated towards the crossing, knowing that she had at least a minute before the train came. She drove to the other side of the railway tracks with at least twenty seconds to spare, did a U-turn and waited until the train passed.

She was now following a different line of thought. Having seen a television program about CPR, she remembered the importance of commencing it as soon as possible, as it only took about three minutes before the brain started dying. It had been at least three minutes since her husband had slumped onto her shoulder but she had to be sure. Waiting for the train to pass would delay her a few more minutes and she couldn't be accused of contributing to his death. She crossed the railway tracks again and slowly drove to her family doctor. He was a sensible sort of chap who wouldn't attempt heroic measures, she thought. After taking her time about parking the car, she went inside to the doctor's receptionist, emphasised that her husband looked very ill and asked if the doctor could see him in the car as she didn't think he'd make it into the surgery by himself. The doctor accompanied Mrs Mathieson to the car and could see even without opening the door that Mr Mathieson was dead. He approached the body from the driver's side and declared him as such.

It was routine in the town that the body had to be taken to the hospital's morgue until funeral arrangements were made. The ambulance arrived and the two paramedics tried to cheer Mrs Mathieson up by asking if she had ever been in an ambulance with the siren on and lights flashing. 'No,' she replied. 'I've never done that.' So she went to the hospital in the back of the ambulance, lights flashing, siren wailing, seated next to her laid-out husband, quietly weeping with that strange combination of relief and grief that many suffer on such occasions.

13
The living will

One unfortunate result of avoiding honest discussions about ageing, dying and death is that when the time comes we may not know the wishes of those close to us. And it may not be a black-and-white issue, especially when the patient is unconscious and you must make a decision based on a projected state of health, with certain prospects of surviving and at a cost in terms of the long-term independence and quality of life of your loved one. Failing to designate others to make those important decisions on your behalf, can be unfair to both your loved ones and yourself. Others may think they know what you would want but that may not actually coincide with your own wishes.

Moreover, they will usually err on the conservative side, opting to continue active treatment, perhaps leaving you surviving in a state that you would never have wanted. Then there is the guilt and anxiety that those making the decisions must shoulder.

Framing choices about your preferences and communicating your values around end of life is known as advanced care planning (ACP), or creating a living will. It is a process whereby a person, often in consultation with healthcare providers, family members and significant others, makes decisions about their future health care should they become incapable of participating in those decisions.

Neil was eighty-four years of age with severe dementia—so severe that he was under the care of psychogeriatricians and required increasing doses of sedation because of his violent behaviour. As a result of him developing a fever and becoming quieter, he was transferred from the psychogeriatric ward to a medical ward in the same hospital.

His problems were:

• A urinary tract infection—potentially treatable.
• A low serum sodium level—potentially treatable.

- Shock—potentially treatable.
- Early renal failure—potentially treatable.
- A blocked airway, caused by a very low level of consciousness—also potentially manageable by placing a tube into his lungs and assisting his breathing with artificial ventilation.

In theory, because all of the abnormalities were treatable, Neil could have all of these problems addressed and maybe he would survive. At best, he would be returned to the psychogeriatric ward in the state he was in before he developed the other problems.

Considering the bigger picture, Neil's dementia was advanced and would deteriorate even further; soon it would be fatal. How soon is difficult to say exactly—weeks, months, perhaps a year or two—but his condition was definitely terminal.

If Neil had discussed the possibility of not wanting to live in a demented state near the end of his life with his loved ones, or even with his doctor, he could have included his wish not to have active management of any complications under those circumstances. When thinking about ACP in case you become cognitively impaired, it is important to emphasise the state of health and level of care that you would find unacceptable, if you were to survive whatever medical interventions were potentially available for your condition. And, in the light of that information, to consider what level of escalation you would find acceptable.

Advanced care planning should cover medical issues but also other preferences, such as organ and tissue donation, your preferred site of death and those whom you would like to be present at your death.

The term advanced care directive (ACD) or living will refers to the document that is constructed around those preferences. Advanced care directives are based on values such as respect, dignity and autonomy. An ACD should be immediately available when a person loses their capacity to make decisions. Advanced care planning would go a long way towards ensuring that you receive the health care you wish for at the end of life. Not surprisingly, there is a lot of scientific evidence to show that ACP results in the wishes of the patients being respected, and that the anxiety and stress of the family members is less than in those who had no ACD. Here are some general guidelines for advanced care planning:

Try to imagine conditions of health that you would find unacceptable

It is important to remember when considering ACP that when you are elderly and becoming frail, aggressive treatment will almost never make you better than your baseline state, or how you were before you became ill. In other words, when constructing the ACD, imagine the state that you might find yourself in before any life-threatening event. Consider whether you would find that state acceptable rather than just concentrating on whether you would wish for any escalation in treatment. To help in understanding the concept of ACP, imagine conditions you would find unacceptable, such as being totally dependent on others for all of your care. Articulate other anxieties, such as a fear of pain and humiliation; loss of dignity; incontinence; and being unable to move without assistance.

Adrian, a seventy-three-year-old man, had a history of heart failure, followed by a heart attack that caused a large clot to form in the heart. The clot broke off, causing a stroke, which resulted in him being confined to bed or a wheelchair and unable to swallow, necessitating a tube for feeding directly into his stomach. He was unable to speak normally but was orientated and aware of his surroundings. Adrian developed a fever and low blood pressure while living in a nursing home. He was rushed to hospital, given antibiotics and intravenous fluids, made a recovery after three days and was discharged back to the nursing home in the same shape he was in before the infection.

Many people might not want to return to that state of dependence. As part of your decision-making you should not view the infection in isolation, as something that is treatable without any further problems. Unfortunately, this is what doctors often do. A serious life-threatening infection can no longer be viewed in isolation. In the elderly frail, a severe infection requiring admission to an ICU can also indicate that you are in line for increasing hospitalisations and are approaching the end of your life. These are population-based observations and obviously cannot be applied accurately in every individual case. However, you need to consider these often complicated situations when constructing your ACP.

Determine whether you would want any treatment if your health suddenly worsened

Imagine states of existence that you would find unacceptable. Write them down or articulate them in some way. Then state what level of treatment you would like if you developed complications or a new disease that might be life-threatening if not treated. Common examples are an infection from the urinary tract, cellulitis (infection of the skin) or pneumonia. Unfortunately—or fortunately—these are easily treated with antibiotics but in severe cases may require hospitalisation for intravenous fluids and life support in an intensive care unit.

Set your own limits around how you would want to be treated if this occurred while you are able. For example, you may opt for antibiotics at home but not hospitalisation. You may choose not to have any antibiotics but to be offered comfort care to alleviate any possible suffering. On the other hand, you may request 'the works'—that everything possible be done.

Let's imagine that you have severe dementia and are likely to develop a urinary tract infection or pneumonia as a life-threatening event. Begin your ACP with a general description of the state of your health that you would find unacceptable before any life-threatening event occurred. For example:

If I was severely demented and no longer able to recognise my loved ones I would want no further active management of any medical complication.

Or:

I would want some active management, e.g. antibiotics in my place of residence, but not to be admitted to hospital.

Or:

I would want to be admitted to hospital to find out exactly what the cause of my deterioration was and to have limited active treatment, e.g. intravenous fluid and antibiotics, but not to be admitted to an ICU for further life support.

Or:

I would want to be urgently transferred to an acute hospital and to be admitted to an ICU if necessary for full life support until the situation was deemed hopeless by the treating physicians.

Other terminal events in frail old age may include a stroke, heart attack or a catastrophe such as an embolism, blocking the vessels supplying the bowel, causing the intestines to die. You may need to construct your wishes around these events, which may be a normal and natural way to die if you are in a state of infirmity that you would not be comfortable with.

For more detail, below are some of the possible escalations of treatment that you should consider:

- Would not like to be admitted to hospital under any circumstance, but to have pain relief and to be made comfortable.
- Would not like to be admitted to hospital if demented or with equivalent degree of permanent brain damage from whatever cause.
- Would only like to be admitted to hospital if there was a high likelihood of being discharged back to the community in a state of health and with a quality of life that was similar to that which you had before hospital admission.
- Would like to be admitted to hospital if there was a large component of the illness that was potentially reversible but would not like to be admitted to the ICU under any circumstance.
- Would like to be admitted to hospital if you developed a life-threatening illness which had a

good chance of successful treatment with only a short period of hospital admission.

- Would like to be admitted to hospital, but if the short period of definitive treatment failed, or a treatment either wasn't going as well as expected or complications set in and you were unlikely to survive hospital and/or you were likely to have a quality of life much lower than before, you would like active treatment withdrawn.

- Would like to be admitted to hospital, but to have all active treatment withdrawn if you were in a state where it was impossible for you ever to make an informed decision by yourself, such as if you were in a persistent vegetative state, in the terminal stages of a disease (the last few hours or days), or suffering from a disease state where you would never return to being able to make an informed decision. In this situation you would also like artificial feeding and fluids ceased and to be made comfortable.

- Would like to be admitted to the ICU, which is a significant step up in treatment complexity, if your illness had a good chance of recovery within a few days and the chances of you returning to the community in the same state that you were in before admission was good.

- Would like to be admitted to the ICU if there was a good chance of recovery to your pre-hospital status but would like treatment limited.
- Would like treatment in the ICU ceased and to be made comfortable and have adequate pain relief if improvement was not occurring or the condition was becoming worse after about five days or more.
- Would like active treatment in the ICU to continue even if there was a high likelihood of your condition being worse after discharge from hospital and probably requiring a higher level of care.
- Would like active treatment in the ICU to continue even when you were not making noticeable progress and there was little hope of recovery.
- Would like treatment in the ICU to continue even when there was little hope of recovery and you would probably require a higher level of care, perhaps in a different setting than when you were admitted, such as in an institution.

In all of these decisions, there will be uncertainty. Uncertainty is an inherent part of medicine. Some people will use it to justify continuing active treatment and others do not want to take the risk of living in a way that would be inconsistent with their wishes, especially when those risks are high. The doubt can turn into greater certainty with time, as you see the effect of a certain combination of therapies.

Examples from life

Rita, an eighty-six-year-old woman living at home, had a pacemaker and had undergone surgery for bowel cancer five years previously. She was admitted with a fistula between the bowel and her vagina, causing a continuous faecal discharge from the vagina. There were two options for her. First, major surgery in order to stop the faecal discharge from her vagina. Second, in view of her age, chronic health status and the possibility that this might be a recurrence of cancer, that she have no major surgery and be treated symptomatically in order to avoid pain or any other suffering.

In this case, Rita was living independently and had a reasonable quality of life. She might be quite happy to be returned to such a state. The decision was whether to live with continuous faecal discharge from her vagina or to have major surgery involving a colostomy, where the faeces is diverted to a bag on the abdominal wall. In either case, she would have to live with faeces being handled in a different way to normal. If the patient is cognitively intact and able to make such a decision, an ACD is not necessary. However, if Rita had developed serious complications, then someone else would have had to make that choice for her. The ACP might help in that decision-making, but it would be difficult to include such specific information being translated into medical action. The ACD is not able to cover every medical contingency. There are too many possibilities and too many 'ifs and buts', and your wishes should be expressed in general lay terms.

David, a seventy-three-year-old man, lived independently with a few medical issues, such as high blood pressure, diabetes and smoking-related decrease in lung function. He was admitted to hospital with a perforation of his gut. He was conscious on admission and, after his condition was explained, he agreed to a colectomy, removing the bowel, which had been perforated.

David was too ill to be taken off life support after his operation and came back to the ICU needing artificial ventilation and powerful drugs to support his circulation. He had developed a life-threatening infection as a result of the perforation. His kidneys had failed, requiring dialysis. The drugs supporting his circulation had to be increased to industrial doses. It looked as if he would not survive.

Discussions were held with his family. It was agreed that there would be no further escalation of treatment but neither would the existing treatment be withdrawn until we had more information.

David was deeply unconscious and so sedation was ceased to ascertain his mental state. Over the next few weeks his condition gradually improved. After three weeks he was awake enough to be taken off life support. Unfortunately, his kidneys never recovered and he required permanent dialysis. This in itself can severely compromise one's quality of life, with repeated admissions to the dialysis unit or having to be dialysed at home with various techniques. It also meant that David's life span was seriously shortened.

How does one cover these complexities with ACP? Does one add this particular possibility to all the other complications that can occur in the aged after a major illness? David decided to have the initial operation, which, under the circumstances, many of us would probably have done. But he suffered complications and, as a result of his illness, was unable to participate in further decision-making. Moreover, while his condition was dire, he may have made an uneventful recovery and returned home for a long period of convalescence. He may have suffered other complications such as a stroke, dead gut as a result of compromised blood supply or a severe heart attack. Maybe the ACP could be worded in generic terms such as: 'In the event of suffering severe complications as a result of a potentially treatable condition, I would not choose to undergo any further active treatment.' However, what if the potentially life-threatening complications could be managed and the chance of total or almost total recovery was possible? David's condition was so severe at one stage that the doctors discussed the high possibility of him not surviving. He did survive, but with a condition that would change his life considerably and he may have regretted his survival under these circumstances.

These possibilities are mentioned only to focus on the shortcomings of ACP in the practical world. This is not to say that they should be abandoned.

Quite the opposite. Even if you cannot anticipate all of the possible situations that may occur when you are unable to make a rational decision yourself, the concept of ACP performs an important function.

Most importantly it means that you have discussed the issue, even in general terms, with those you trust. In case you do become incompetent, your loved ones will not be forced to make these decisions entirely by themselves. Otherwise, where there is even the smallest doubt, they are likely to opt for active treatment, which may not coincide with your own wishes. Those of us working in intensive care see the anguish and guilt in relatives who must try to anticipate what you may have wanted and are reluctant to be seen as heartless if they say, 'This is not what they would have wanted—I suggest we stop all active treatment.'

Robert, an eighty-three-year-old man, fell off a ladder while changing a light bulb. Falls can be a terminal event in the elderly (see chapter 4). Robert had multiple fractured ribs but had been previously living independently with his wife. Without artificial ventilation, Robert probably would have died. With it, he was in the ICU for three days before he was taken off the ventilator. He left hospital five days later much the same as he was before he fell, apart from being banned by his wife from all future ladder use. If he had put in his ACP that he never wanted to be in an ICU on a ventilator, he wouldn't have lived. At the same time, falls and hospitalisation are powerful predictors of failing health.

The above cases emphasise just how difficult it is to account for every contingency in an ACD. These complexities are almost impossible to capture in words.

Tips for those undertaking advanced care planning

- **The role of an ACD**: It is important to remember that the ACD would only be required when you are not cognitively capable of expressing your wishes.
- **Unacceptable states of living**: Try to define what you would find as an unacceptable state of living and in what circumstances you wouldn't want *any* further active treatment of any sort, e.g. if you had advanced dementia or were bed-bound and totally dependent on others for all support.
- **Do not attempt resuscitation (DNAR) or Not for Resuscitation (NFR)**: It is often thought that it is important to state whether you would prefer CPR

when your heart stops. CPR can be effective when you have a sudden arrhythmia, such as ventricular fibrillation, and when it is witnessed and responded to by skilled personnel. However, this does not happen when you are dying as a result of a terminal illness such as cancer or even just because you are elderly and frail. In these circumstances, CPR will almost never be effective and it would be perverse even to administer the treatment to someone who is predictably and naturally dying. While popular in the lay media and often discussed even by hospital physicians, these orders miss the point. When a DNAR or NFR order is being considered, it is time to discuss the issue of dying and how you would want the process to be managed in the broad sense of the meaning. It is time to consider issues such as the prognosis and expected course of your illness; your preferences with regard to treatment limitations; where you would like to be managed; what support will be necessary to support that process; if that support will be available; and many other issues. Fill in the DNAR form if you wish, but also be aware of the wider and more important implications inherent in this discussion.

- **Terminal disease**: In the event of nearing the end when you have a terminal disease such as cancer or motor neurone disease, you may not wish for further escalation of active treatment. These are usually illnesses where your cognitive function is intact and you can continue to make rational choices. However, you need to state your wishes in case there are complications which preclude you from making rational choices.
- **When things go wrong**: In the course of any operation or treatment there may be complications which make recovery very unlikely. In that event, depending on the level of complication and what it means for your future health, you may prefer the following courses of action:
  - No further escalation of active treatment.
  - Further escalation until the poor outcome becomes even more likely.
  - Continued treatment until your body gives out despite all active attempts to treat you.
  - Accepting the high probability of poor quality of life even if discharged from hospital alive.
- **Quality of life after hospital discharge**: When you are elderly and becoming increasingly frail,

there are certain illnesses, such as serious life-threatening infections and falls, which may require you to be admitted to an ICU and be put on life support if you are to survive. However, in many such cases your need for such support may be an indication that your reserves are decreased and, without drastic interventions, you may not live. Even if you survive, there is now evidence your quality of life may be severely impaired after you are discharged back to the community. You may like to add a general statement in your ACD, along the lines of: 'In the event that I suffer a serious illness requiring life support or repeated hospitalisations and it is likely that my quality of life would significantly decrease and my dependence on others would increase then . . .' And state your wish.

- **An ACD is a dynamic document**: Your ACD may change during your lifetime for many different reasons. You may be suffering pain and decreased mobility in a way that is becoming more unacceptable and so you may wish to adjust your ACP wishes to have a lower threshold for declining further active treatment. Alternatively, what you felt would be an unacceptable state of living at some time in your life is something that you have adjusted to and now you would wish to have more aggressive attempts to be kept alive even if it is not in a state you would have found acceptable when you were younger and in better health.

- **Medical input**: If possible, design your ACP with the assistance of someone with medical knowledge, ideally your family practitioner. They can identify some technical issues and translate some of your choices into medical language where necessary.

- **Financial and personal planning**: It is wise to complete a living will about your medical wishes together with an enduring power of attorney document which similarly covers your financial and personal wishes. 'Elder abuse' is becoming more common around the world. There are some who would take advantage of your diminishing abilities to undertake financial planning as ageing occurs. Try to discuss the issues with trusted family or friends in order to avoid future confrontations and relationship breakdowns.

- **'No heroic measures in the face of futility'**: If you haven't got around to a more complex documentation of your wishes, even a simple statement such as this would give doctors an idea of your wishes. Sign it and put it in your wallet.

- **Make a recording**: It is a good idea to make a recording of your wishes, both audio and visual, perhaps surrounded by your family or other trusted people who, more than likely, will be helping to make decisions should you become incompetent. In this way the hospital health team can get a more personal sense of you and your wishes.

Looking ahead

While ACPs are important for individuals, the way we deliver health care needs to realigned. Currently health care is roughly divided into prevention, cure and rehabilitation. A new era should include systematic measures to accommodate an ageing population and patient-centred end-of-life care. Part of the reorganisation of health delivery would involve breaking down the existing silo-based care which makes it difficult for patients to negotiate the boundaries between general practice, hospitals and community care. These silos do not usually communicate well and patients fall between the gaps. Instead, we should create targeted packages focused on patient needs, coordinating community, nursing, paramedical, ambulance, hospital and specialist medical services. Inbuilt into these systems is the need for carer support and respite care.

In summary, it is difficult to encapsulate every preference given the myriad possible clinical contingencies at the end of life. For nit-picking lawyers, the ACD would always have weaknesses when translating the preferences into clinical decision-making. It is probably preferable to state your wishes in broad terms, trying to anticipate the status of health dependence and quality of life that you would find acceptable, rather than document every medical possibility and the choice you would make under these circumstances. A flexible patient-centred approach may ensure a patient's autonomy to self-determination is respected. There are many ACP and ACD guidelines available for expressing preferences. Spare a thought for the potentially serious problems that arise for relatives who have had to make decisions about the end-of-life care of patients when there was no ACP.

Patient autonomy is a fundamental right of people when deciding what health care they want. There is no reason to deny the right of the individual to make their own choices about their own health care. Our society should be given a lot more information about the prognosis of the elderly frail and the possible trajectories of their future health. This would ensure that ACP is based on more reliable information. The current system virtually ensures that the treatment given to those patients at the end of life without explicit ACDs will not follow the patient's preferences, at great cost to society and to people suffering futile treatment, not consistent with their own wishes.

Tips for governments and health service providers

There are actions governments and health service providers could take to better address the needs of patients at the end of life. To begin with, they could divert some of the research funds for curing conditions such as cancer and dementia into research to identify more accurately the prognosis of people coming to the end of life; establishing systems so that these people, once identified, are informed in an honest and compassionate way; identifying their choices once armed with that knowledge; and determining whether the services related to these choices are available.

In addition, they could establish services for the elderly frail and terminally ill people that are consistent with their wishes. Initially this will involve extra expenditure, but there is a strong possibility that once these services are developed and available, the need for expensive acute hospital services would decrease. However, it would be a mistake to close the acute hospital services without first establishing alternative support, consistent with people's wishes. Public health campaigns (similar to successful preventative medicine campaigns such as AIDS, smoking and wearing seat belts) could be encouraged to create practical support around ageing and dying in a more honest and transparent way. And we should ensure that the law and medical practice are consistent with ensuring that people's wishes are respected and enacted.

14
Giving up the ghost

How did we get to a situation where an increasing number of our elderly will spend their last few days in an intensive care unit supported by complex machinery at a cost of at least AUD$4000 per patient per day? Most patients would prefer to die in their own home; most doctors do not want to be treated themselves in an ICU at the end of their life; and the cost is one of the largest contributors to the unsustainable costs of health care. How did ageing and dying become so medicalised?

Nobody planned it and it's not in the interest of our society. It just happened and we have all collaborated and contributed in different ways.

First, our attitudes and beliefs around modern medicine provide fertile ground for the medicalisation of ageing and dying. There are daily reports of medical miracles, even from the most responsible media. Our society wants to believe in cures and the medical profession does little to put the latest miracle in perspective. Most people, including doctors, grossly overestimate the positive impact of medicine on health-related conditions and, at the same time, underestimate the harm.

There are millions being spent on research around fighting the ageing process, so that rich folk from developed societies can live longer. Some entrepreneurs are even working on living forever. There is arguably more money spent on fighting ageing in developed countries than on providing basic health care to millions in poorer countries.

Ageing and dying have become taboo subjects and are not discussed openly. The discussions are around how to 'fight' it rather than on how to accept and come to terms with it. Ageing and dying are no longer normal processes to be accepted as inevitable. Anti-ageing creams, tablets, diets and surgical procedures abound as people are dragged kicking and screaming through the ageing process, comparing themselves with others, hungrily accepting compliments about their appearance and spending a fortune on snake oil remedies.

Against this background, it is difficult for doctors to be open and honest about the prognosis of their patients, surrounded by impressive-looking machines. I struggle with this every day in the ICU. The constant reports of medical miracles are extrapolated to the bedside of the dying patient, making it difficult for me to explain, and for the public to accept, that nothing more can be done.

The medical profession is not an innocent bystander. This approach to medical teaching and practice was designed before so many people started living to a ripe old age. It was designed around relatively young people having a single medical problem. Elderly people in the village were rare. Over the last few decades, the life span in developed countries has increased. There are now many of us living to an age undreamt of several decades ago. Huge industries are being built around the ageing population. Whole walls of pharmaceutical products abound with aids for incontinence and for getting around without falling. Aged care facilities are one of the fastest-growing industries in developed countries.

Medical specialisation developed at a time when younger patients often had a single organ problem, deserving of a specific diagnostic label. Built around this simplistic notion was a medical specialist to match your single problem. However, nowadays, most hospitalised patients are old, with multiple age-related problems that are not confined to one organ.

Specialists are trained to incrementally fine-tune their own bit of the body. They have little insight into how their bit may affect and be affected by the overall clinical picture of an aged person at the end of their life. Most cannot stand back, see the big picture and be honest with patients and their carers about their possible limited life span and how they would like to spend it.

A patient's clinical condition is still assigned according to organ-related definitions. It is inferred that the individual organ problems can all be treated independently by the various organ specialists. It is mainly a question of luck which organ specialist the elderly will be admitted under on presentation to an acute hospital. Once you have been randomly assigned to one organ specialist, you will be referred to other colleagues in order to address all the other problems associated with ageing organs. You will accumulate your own committee of physicians. However, like many committees, it will have no overall agenda, strategic direction or action plan.

There is also subtle pressure on the various organ specialists to not underestimate the impact of their own contribution to a patient's wellbeing even if they are near the end of their life. They don't want to be the odd man out on the committee and suggest to others that what we are doing is futile and possibly giving a cruel sense of false hope.

As a result, the number of pills you are on will multiply. The number of pills is a reflection of where you are in life and, often, how close you may be to the end. Some enlightened doctors just stop the lot as the end draws near. This move has some scientific merit, as the effectiveness of the drugs in the elderly frail coming to the end of their lives has never been established; trials usually focus on a younger population with few other medical problems. If one was a cynic one might suggest that it is not in the pharmaceutical industry's interest to undertake trials on the elderly with confounding issues such as the interaction of all the other drugs they are taking; their changing metabolism; and the way that drugs are handled in the elderly. It might just cast doubt on exactly what impact all these pills have on the health of the elderly.

Doctors are not trained to work within this new paradigm of elderly patients with multiple age-related co-morbidities at the end of their life. They know that people die but they are programmed to diagnose, treat and sometimes cure. This is deeply embedded in their attitudes, beliefs and the way they practise their craft. There is little emphasis in medical training on accepting ageing and dying as a natural and inevitable process and being honest with their patients and carers. Hope and reassurance are important to both the patient and doctors and this need often trumps reality.

Hope clashes with uncertainty and uncertainty is an integral part of medicine. Certainty is rare. Where there is uncertainty, there is hope. A disease process can take many different forms. The effectiveness of treatment is often unpredictable, depending on factors such as when the condition was detected, when treatment was started and the underlying condition of the host. And that is just for a single disease with a proven treatment.

Uncertainty is also inherent in the elderly frail patient with multiple age-related conditions. We are never too sure how long they have to live or when they will begin to lose their independence nor how steep the deterioration trajectory will be. Deterioration in the elderly is related more to the sum of the individual clinical problems associated with ageing as much, if not more than, say, the bladder infection which resulted in the patient presenting to hospital. Bladder infections are easy to treat but the underlying so-called co-morbidities are as a result of natural ageing and are relatively resistant to cures. Thus it is easier and possibly justified to concentrate only on the bladder infection and ignore the overall clinical condition of the patient, how close they may be to death and what their wishes may be. Acute infections such as pneumonia allowed elderly patients to die with dignity, pain-free and with little suffering. Nowadays, patients with acute infections are often seen in the ICU on a ventilator, being dialysed and aggressively resuscitated in order to treat the infection of the lung.

Individuals and societies will approach uncertainty in different ways. Uncertainty may be used legally and ethically to justify continuing to support someone in an ICU. It is common for relatives to say to me, 'Are you certain Mum will die?' I then try to be honest about the likelihood of death and introduce the chances of future deterioration and quality of life even if the patient were to survive. Often I am met with questions and statements along the lines of: 'But if we leave her on life support there may be a miracle. We've all heard of miracles happening.' And: 'Doctors are not always right.' And: 'But Mum has always been a fighter— there's a good chance she'll pull through. She's done it before.' You can understand why, at this point, doctors will continue treatment.

Sometimes people pray for God to save their relative. This can also be difficult for the treating team. In these circumstances, my explanation might be along the lines that life support machines are artificial. They are not the way God made us to live. Stopping the machines will put the patient's life in God's hands. If it is God's will, the person will live. A miracle does not need life support machines.

There are many ways of being honest about the uncertainty without neglecting the certainty. We know there are certain indicators that indicate a patient may be coming to the end of their life, including weight loss, being totally confined to bed and an increasing dependency on others for feeding, washing and toileting. This adds up to a condition called 'frailty', discussed in chapter 11. The term frailty is starting to be recognised in medicine. It may even eventually attain the status of being a syndrome, which is a cluster of signs and symptoms found in patients. This, in turn, may encourage more attention and research and help to add some certainty to the uncertainty.

Although doctors cannot predict the exact day of death, I try to explain that there will be further inevitable deterioration even if the patient were to survive and be discharged from the ICU. I then try to insert into the discussions enquiries about the patient's own wishes, should they end up being on life support in an ICU. A living will can help here.

There are also ethical drivers that make honest discussion about death and dying difficult. The specialty of intensive care has meant that we can delay death even when it is inevitable with the support provided by the machines and drugs. The four ethical principles underpinning the practice of medicine are beneficence (doing good), non-maleficence (doing no harm), autonomy (respecting patient's wishes) and the broader concept of justice or how the treatment is seen in the context of the whole society.

They are laudable principles and ones that are difficult to argue with. However, the principles were delivered like the Ten Commandments by ethicists with little insight into their practical application. Like the Ten Commandments, they came from on high with little apparent input from practising clinicians and the community. A good example of an ethical dilemma, and one that I'm often faced with, is withdrawing and/or withholding treatment from patients on life support in an ICU and where there is no longer hope of recovery.

Autonomy acknowledges the wishes of the patient and their carers. Autonomy may be the right of a patient to make choices about their health. However, as is often the case in the ICU, the patient is unable to make decisions and a surrogate is consulted. For many reasons the surrogate may demand that full treatment in the ICU be continued indefinitely, even if the patient is in their nineties, demented, living in an institution and totally dependent on others for all their needs. Even when the patient's heart eventually stops of its own accord, the surrogate may demand that full resuscitative measures, including CPR, be instituted for an indefinite time. The wishes of the relatives in this case may clash with the wider social justice issue. Can we justify spending AUD$4000 a day on continuing to keep this person alive when there is almost no hope that they would survive the withdrawal of support? (There is that uncertainty again—'almost'.) The high cost of keeping one person alive may be translated into alternative ways of allocating that health resource into areas such as community support for patients in their own homes and assistance for the army of carers who currently have little in the way of support and scant opportunities for respite care, or more resources for improved public health measures.

Beneficence can also be applied in different and conflicting ways. Some would argue that it is good to sustain life at all costs. Others would argue that it is not in the patient's interest to prolong someone's suffering in the face of futility and to give relatives false hope of a patient's survival. Ariel Sharon, a former prime minister of Israel, suffered a stroke that left him in a persistent vegetative state, or coma, from which he would never recover. Nevertheless, he remained on full life support in an ICU for eight years. Were we 'doing good' for Ariel Sharon?

Similarly, non-maleficence, or 'doing no harm', could be interpreted as avoiding harm by reducing the suffering of the patient by discontinuing futile care as well as minimising the suffering of the family that feels responsible for keeping their loved one alive when there is no hope of recovery.

The ethical principles are meant to offer a guide to medical practice. However, they have little practical application in the context of withdrawing and withholding treatment. Without further guidelines to explain how to achieve a practical balance, the principles, because of their flexible interpretation, are almost meaningless. They not only offer little practical assistance to treating physicians, they can be used to justify almost any action.

Similarly, the law has great difficulty in nailing down specific guidelines around withdrawing and withholding treatment in the face of futility in an ICU. Moreover, each society has varying religious, cultural and historical influences informing their laws.

It is difficult to construct unequivocal laws around the already slippery ethical concepts in attempting to define what is 'right'. How can rigidly constructed laws claim to reflect the rights and wrongs of protecting patients and their carers, the treating clinicians and society as a whole? Laws attempting to give some generic and broad guidelines may face the same problems encountered in applying the four ethical principles, where they are so general as to be of little value.

Some countries may see withdrawing treatment of an elderly frail person supported by sophisticated machines as taking a life and therefore prohibited by law. Other countries may emphasise the rights of the patient and their choice. Others may include the rights of doctors to refuse to deliver futile treatment. And other countries simply cannot afford ICUs and direct their resources to the more basic needs of people.

Many countries are now acknowledging that detailed prescriptive laws are not applicable in these circumstances and attempt to take a flexible and broad approach. The diagnosis of imminent death is basically a medical one. The most practical next steps involve sensitive discussions between the physician, patient and, in the case of patients supported in an ICU, the patient's family and carers. In many countries, the law is increasingly attempting to construct broad principles around this approach.

The fear of litigation is one that doctors may use in order to justify continuing to support active treatment in the face of futility. However, litigation would only be possible if patients and their carers are given false expectations as to the likely outcome of continuing futile treatment. In fact, litigation could be used as a tool to prevent inappropriate treatment without full disclosure of the possible outcomes of such treatment in the short, medium and long term.

More important than the so-called ethical principles and the law is creating an ICU where end-of-life care is seen as core business, not something that's done reluctantly. Where it is essential to speak plainly, avoiding specialist medical terms and evasive language. We need to judge an ICU on the way it cares for those who die as much as we do for those who survive.

Then there is the elephant in the room. In health systems where doctors are paid on the basis of services delivered rather than receiving a salary, there is an incentive to provide services. The more tests and interventions, the higher the remuneration. Elderly patients at the end of life are a potentially rich source of complex and expensive interventions. The escalation of treatment may involve inserting intravenous lines, delivering expensive drugs, establishing artificial ventilation, commencing haemodialysis and many other interventions, each carrying a large fee for service. The treatment can be easily justified on the basis of uncertainty and by playing on the emotions of the relatives who, when asked about the next steps in the escalation, would usually agree with the doctor, rather than be seen as the one who was responsible for ending the patient's life. Many Americans become bankrupt in the process of keeping a relative alive in the face of futility.

If a physician earns his living by doing things, then it is obvious that they will be more likely to do them. It would be reassuring to say otherwise, but it is the system within which the clinician operates that largely determines the perverse incentive for doctors. This may not be in the patient's interest, nor in the interest of relatives who have to pay the bill, nor the society which has to devote more of the limited resources it has to health.

The cost of health care in the last six months of life is astronomical. We imagine that palliative care aims to allow people to die with dignity and without suffering. Most of us would be surprised to learn that the word 'palliative' is also applied to active and expensive interventions such as 'palliative' surgery or 'palliative' chemotherapy. Some of the so-called 'palliative surgery' may be to reduce pain or suffering. However, most of these 'palliative' interventions are attempting to give the patient a few extra weeks or months of life, no matter what extra suffering it may cause. An example would be the powerful drug Sipuleucel-T, given to cancer patients with metastatic spread of their tumour. At best it may prolong life by three to five months and has all the usual side effects of chemotherapy. It costs AUD$93,000 per course. On the other hand, it has been estimated that community-based palliative care delivered in the person's home for the last three months of life would cost $6000.

Inherent in every doctor's training is the need to prevent death. Active interventions at the end of life are usually sold to patients on the basis that they will delay the inevitable, but with little explanation of the extra suffering they may cause. Delaying the inevitable

216

is an attractive option if one is dying but the option is not usually explained in an objective way. Most doctors, when asked about further active treatment towards the end of their own lives and when death is inevitable, would not opt for aggressive treatment. Yet these same doctors recommend that their patients should undergo such treatment. (A common joke doing the rounds goes something like this: 'Why do they nail down the lids of coffins? To prevent the oncologist from giving further chemotherapy.')

A further irony results from a landmark study that showed patients who chose palliative care and aggressive treatment lived longer with a better quality of life than those who were subject to aggressive end-of-life treatment alone.

What are the practical drivers that result in many of the elderly spending their last few days or weeks of life in acute hospitals being supported on machines in ICUs?

People at the end of life are put on a conveyor belt. The combination of chronic failing health finally tips them into a zone where they become seriously ill as a result of a minor problem, such as a urinary tract infection on top of the multiple age-related problems, resulting in them easing into the final stages of life.

In times past, ageing would have followed a natural and predictable course over several decades. When an elderly person developed an infection, they would have been made comfortable, usually in their own home, and within hours or days would have drifted to the end of their life with dignity, surrounded by acceptance and sadness.

Now, as that time approaches and the patient becomes seriously ill in the community, an ambulance is usually called. It takes them to the nearest emergency department, which is focused on immediate resuscitation then packaging and delivering the patient to the most appropriate place for further care. In many cases it is easier to admit the elderly patient to the hospital for treatment. Depending on the level of illness, they may then end up in the ICU for the final few hours or days of life. To emphasise the current failure of this approach it is sobering to know that one-third of all emergency calls within hospitals are for patients at the end of life. In other words, hospitals often do not recognise terminally ill patients.

The system is constructed around the conveyor belt. You often will not be recognised as dying until you are within hours or days of death. It is currently difficult for one person or health professional to pluck you off the conveyor belt and give you and your family an honest assessment of the situation. You are deprived of the opportunity to exercise choices about how you want to spend your last few weeks or months of life. The machine operating the conveyor belt would have taken over.

15
Futility

If death is a medical failure then medicine
is a doomed art.

Julian Sheather, *Life Before Death*

For all its clever technology, one of the most difficult dilemmas facing modern medicine is obtaining accurate information about when conventional medicine becomes futile. As is the case for most of medicine, there is often little in the way of certainty. When making a decision to let someone die, the uncertainty often leads to prolonged life support even when there is little hope. 'Little hope' . . . When does 'little hope' become 'no hope'? Once there is 'no hope,' then further treatment is futile.

It is very difficult for medicine to declare there is 'no hope'. Someone whose brain has ceased functioning is an exception. Even then, there are some who insist that the heart has to stop and breathing cease before death is pronounced. This overlooks the fact that breathing has ceased when the brain has died, and if it were not for the artificial machines 'life' would cease. But let's put this aside, as the majority of society has accepted the concept of brain death equating with death.

However, there are many elderly frail patients also being supported in intensive care units whose condition has little in the way of reversibility. Sometimes the 'little hope' can be replaced by 'no hope', but often only after days, weeks or months of active management in an ICU. In the meantime, the patient continues to deteriorate further until, even with maximum technology, they just drift away and die.

Our research group has recently published data suggesting that up to one-third of all interventions in the last twelve months of life are 'non-beneficial' or 'futile', assuming that the interventions were meant to improve the patient's state of health. These interventions excluded interventions that were aimed at reducing pain or unpleasant symptoms. Some prefer the term 'non-beneficial treatment' or 'inappropriate care' to 'futile treatment', but all imply that further active or conventional treatment would not have any effect. Sometimes there is certainty here and that makes it easy, but there is usually some uncertainty. So maybe non-beneficial treatment, when it relates to end-of-life care in the ICU, could be defined as treatment given when the patient would never be able to survive outside an ICU. But, while this helps, there may still be some uncertainty around the idea of 'never' when making a decision to withdraw active treatment.

Another way of looking at terms such as 'futile treatment' or 'non-beneficial treatment' may be to replace them with descriptions, such as 'when the burden of treatment far outweighs any benefit'. This provides some basis for further discussion but we still have a relative term—'far'—which could invite discussion.

You can see that confusion and uncertainty remain around these terms. The description I am coming round to is 'when the burden of treatment would never achieve the patient's goals'. There is room for contemplation and discussion here. Moreover, it is centred around the patient, and not theoretical, philosophical and ethical constructs.

Atul Gawande, the well-known American surgeon and author, uses the phrase 'fatally ill', describing the fatally ill patient as one who has exhausted the potential of scientifically based curative therapy and thus it is just a matter of time before nature takes its course. There remains an implied certainty about the term 'fatally ill'.

Gawande, assuming certainty, suggests that when a person is determined to be 'fatally ill,' four questions should be asked:

1. What is your understanding of your current health or condition?
2. What are your fears?
3. Are there any trade-offs you are willing to make or not?
4. What would a good day be like?

These questions are an excellent way of progressing discussions once we have decided that the person is 'fatally ill' and no treatment would be beneficial. It is certainly relevant for patients with terminal conditions such as cancer. This is an area that has been extensively discussed and researched, resulting in a great deal of certainty. The more pressing situation nowadays is the incremental treatment of the elderly frail, eventually reaching a situation where their relatively minor infection or surgical procedure is not the problem. It is the underlying poor state of the person's general health.

While concentrating on the minor problem we overlook the aged and vulnerable body which would have, in previous years, just passed peacefully away. Now, they are on life support machines and unable to answer Gawande's four very sensible questions.

There are two obvious solutions to the dilemma of how to discuss futility. The first, and obviously preferable one, is to have the patient outline their wishes along the lines proposed by Gawande before serious illness sets in and renders them unable to express those wishes. This notion of advanced care planning is discussed in more detail in chapter 13.

The other way is to have a surrogate explain what they believe the patient's wishes and goals would have been. This is less satisfactory, as it puts the friends and family in a highly stressful situation, where they may feel or be made to feel that they hold the person's life in their hands.

The woman in bed 5, Mrs Hinds, had been admitted overnight. She was seventy-five years old and presented with severe heart failure as a result of her coronary arteries being blocked. The heart failure caused fluid to build up in her lungs, causing shortness of breath and distress. She settled down with some diuretic, a bit of intravenous morphine and CPAP, a device that delivers a small amount of pressurised oxygen via a tight-fitting mask, which in turn assists the breathing. All good so far. Her ECG showed that she was suffering the early stages of a heart attack, confirmed by blood tests. A blocked artery can be unblocked which, in turn, could make the heart work better. She was urgently transferred to the angiography suite, where a total occlusion of one of her coronary arteries was demonstrated. The blockage was overcome with a stent, which squashes the clot against the vessel wall, allowing blood to start flowing to the heart muscle. Otherwise she would have had a full-blown 'heart attack' or 'myocardial infarction', resulting in a large part of her already compromised heart dying.

The stent worked well. Mrs Hinds was on a ventilator, heavily sedated, receiving drugs to keep her blood pressure up and to stop the stent clotting, and her circulation being supported by an intra-aortic balloon pump. The pump is connected to a large catheter inserted into her aorta and pushed up towards the heart. A balloon inflates when the heart is not pumping to help perfuse the coronary arteries and deflates when the heart pumps blood into the aorta around the catheter. The sudden deflation of the balloon may assist the heart to pump more effectively.

This is probably ideal treatment if her problems were confined to the heart. However, she was seventy-five years old, had breast cancer, was riddled with metastases from the cancer and was under palliative care.

How do such things happen? How could anyone advise the patient and their family to undergo such a journey when there is little or no hope of a happy ending? How did an old woman with terminal cancer and not long to live end up receiving this futile treatment?

Long before I became a doctor, in fact long before I attended high school, a next-door neighbour had an operation. I think it was for some sort of cancer in the abdomen. She was elderly and the wife of a retired policeman. My mother used to spend some time with her and we once went on holidays together. I came home from school one day to find my mother in tears; Mrs Blackwell had died in hospital. Apparently she died under the anaesthetic. When the surgeons opened her abdomen, they found that the cancer had spread everywhere. Nowadays that would have been found with sophisticated imaging before the operation and it would have been obvious that further treatment was futile. Futility could be defined with certainty in those days as there were no further treatment options— there was no chemotherapy, radiotherapy or intensive care. So futility depends on the state of what medicine has to offer as well as the clinical state of the patient.

I remember other stories in which people had exploratory operations to confirm spreading cancer and they died under the anaesthetic. No post-operative pain, no suffering in the last few days or weeks of life. With my knowledge now, I doubt the patient was so ill they couldn't cope with the effect of the anaesthetic. I suspect that the patient was allowed to die under the anaesthetic, as there were no further treatment options and the patient would have been subjected to a painful post-operative period with further suffering. Further treatment would have been considered futile and the patient was allowed to die—the way we manage pets with terminal conditions when we don't want them to suffer. We may never know, even if we examined anaesthetic and operation charts from the 1950s and 1960s.

Stephen Streat is an intensive care specialist colleague from Auckland, New Zealand. I admire the incisiveness of his mind and the compassionate way he practises medicine. He emphasises the importance of language when discussing concepts such as futility. Futility implies a lack of worth and perhaps could be interpreted as describing the way the physician views the patient. He reminds us that the term is almost always subjective. Whatever the word, there is a need to be more honest with people, to explain the risks and benefits in a more transparent way and not to underestimate the unnecessary suffering that well-intentioned doctors often inflict on people. People would accept that explanation as readily as they would accept attempts to maintain life at all costs.

16

Intensive care: the beginning of the end

The specialty of intensive care is considered to have been established in Copenhagen in the early 1950s during the poliomyelitis epidemic. Polio affects the body's muscles, causing temporary paralysis which can also have longer-lasting effects. Being unable to move one's limbs effectively is not usually life-threatening, however, when the diaphragm muscles become paralysed you can no longer breathe or cough effectively, resulting in death.

An anaesthetist, Bjorn Ibsen, suggested to Henry Lassen, the physician who cared for these patients, that he could artificially take over the patients' breathing with techniques that he regularly used in the operating rooms. This involved inserting a rubber tube between the vocal cords into the lungs and artificially inflating them with a bellows-type system. They could thus replace the diaphragm's function until the poliomyelitis abated and natural breathing could resume. There were no artificial ventilators in the early 1950s and so Ibsen had medical students work in shifts to squeeze a distensible bag to inflate the lungs and then allow expiration. Soon after, Scandinavia developed and manufactured artificial ventilators which took over the role of the medical students and which today can deliver the breaths in a complex array of patterns according to the patient's needs.

From those beginnings, the specialty of intensive care spread around the world. It developed its own space in the hospital. Doctors and nurses formed specialties with their own research, textbooks, training and qualifications. By the 1970s most large hospitals in the developed world had their own intensive care unit.

Initially intensive care units managed young patients with life-threatening diseases who could potentially recover and return to the community to lead relatively normal lives. These types of patients included those with trauma or severe infections. It was at a time when other specialties, such as cardiac surgery, were undertaking operations which required life support after the operation was completed and until the patient recovered their own breathing and cardiovascular function. These units had many names, such as intensive care units or critical care units. Usually patients only stayed in the unit for a day or two. Then other major surgery became possible as a result of being able to maintain the patient on temporary life support until they recovered. Patients who were suffering severe infections or the effect of overdoses could also be kept alive in the intensive care unit until they recovered. In many cases, recovery was total and the patient who would have otherwise died returned to the community.

The early days of intensive care were exciting. We were the founders of a new specialty, exploring its limits and developing new and innovative ways of supporting life until recovery occurred. We described new illnesses, such as adult respiratory disease syndrome (ARDS), which hadn't existed before we were able to artificially prolong life. We pushed these limits with powerful drugs and machines. The focus was on challenging the existing boundaries of medicine. As a result, the specialty became an integral part of the hospital. Other specialties, such as neurosurgery, cardiac surgery, trauma and many medical specialties, came to depend on intensive care units to keep their patients alive while either nature or their own interventions did their work.

In the rush to push boundaries and develop even more ways to maintain life, we overlooked crucial questions, such as: Whose lives should we be prolonging? What degree of potential reversibility of the illness should be present before we embark on prolongation of life? And what is the patient's long-term outcome likely to be? In other words, just because people were seriously ill and would otherwise die, should we admit them to an intensive care unit for the last few days or weeks of life? If it became apparent that they were not going to survive, what were the laws and society's attitude around ceasing treatment?

How were decisions about withholding and/or withdrawing treatment to be made? Was it entirely the patient's or their carer's choice? Was it based on doctor's advice? What if there was an impasse—how was it to be resolved? What were the laws around this new territory?

In the excitement of becoming a legitimate and highly regarded specialty with unique skills, we were ignoring many of the implications of what we had created.

It wasn't a conspiracy, nor was it something that either society or those working in the specialty necessarily wanted. It just crept up on us and it wasn't until later that some began to stand back and objectively consider the role of intensive care and how we could begin discussions with the community about our work, both its objectives and its limitations.

Meanwhile, our specialty began to change as the population of patients we treated changed. They were no longer young, otherwise fit people who had suffered a catastrophic and life-threatening event. Patients had become older and frailer and were being admitted with a minor illness, such as a fall or infection. The fall or infection was often the result of being elderly and frail. In addition, patients' level of illness and failure to recover was related more to their underlying chronic health status. A fractured bone or infection is straightforward in a twenty-year-old but potentially fatal in the elderly frail.

As the population aged, the number of elderly people requiring emergency calls by ambulance personnel increased at a similar rate, as did admissions to hospital and intensive care. Intensive care has become the place where you are likely to die. Because we could keep younger people alive in the intensive care unit while they recovered, we applied the same complex technology to the elderly. As a result, the incidence of the elderly frail being admitted to intensive care is rising disproportionately at enormous cost both financially and in the suffering of patients and their carers at the end of their lives.

Septicaemia or severe life-threatening infection is the bread and butter of intensive care. Treatment costs run into the billions. We are good at treating septicaemia in the intensive care unit: antibiotics, intravenous fluids, drugs to support the circulation and sometimes more complex interventions such as artificial ventilation and dialysis. As a result, the mortality from septicaemia in intensive care is falling. This is cause for celebration only if you focus on your own small part of the health system. Our thinking and research usually focuses only on what we do in the intensive care unit and on patient outcomes for the limited time we are involved in their care. We could keep the elderly alive in the intensive care units and we could all congratulate each other and publish the results of the miracles in prestigious journals.

But what we do in intensive care is not just about medical miracles. When one looks at the concept of torture there are some frightening similarities to what we inflict unknowingly on patients in the intensive care unit, including isolation, pain, degradation, constant light and sleep deprivation. All sorts of strategies are used by staff to improve conditions for patients, but patients can still be perceived as a set of numbers—a combination of diseases with abnormal pathophysiology.

The difference between genuine torture and what may happen to a patient in the intensive care unit is that staff do not deliberately inflict suffering on patients; quite the opposite. I have never come across any staff in the intensive care unit who wasn't caring and well-meaning. Nevertheless, patients in intensive care suffer many of the things that happen to those who have experienced a severe traumatic event, independent of the illness they were being treated for. We ask too much of our hospitals. They are not a place to die.

Many patients who experience more than a few days in the intensive care unit suffer from hallucinations towards the end of their stay. The hallucinations are often persecutory, related to a fear of staff, and are very frightening. They have usually gone by the time of discharge from hospital. But after discharge from hospital, many patients suffer both physical and psychological damage. Some of the physical changes are predictable: scars where the invasive catheters, tubes and drains were inserted; hair loss; brittle nails; and weight loss with resulting stretch marks. Other problems are less readily visible. Most patients who have been seriously ill and treated in the intensive care unit for more than a few days have profound muscle wasting and weakness, often making even simple tasks, such as walking without assistance, difficult. Joints can become stiff and even 'frozen'. Usually this improves with time, but in some cases the weakness and disability is permanent.

Perhaps even more concerning is the psychological impact. This is the largely unknown world that patients surviving the intensive care unit can experience. Up to half of all patients have anxiety attacks and depression. Many patients suffer serious agoraphobia and have difficulty returning to work or socialising. A significant number have sexual dysfunction and marital breakdowns. As a result of the serious emotional and cognitive impairment many have a decreased ability to manage their household affairs and finance.

Even less acknowledged is the burden on the family and carers. Many patients who have been admitted with a serious illness, such as a stroke or heart attack, have well-organised rehabilitation programs. Rehabilitation programs have many advantages but they rarely exist for patients who have been in intensive care. There are a handful of concerned intensivists who have established clinics to try to provide the unfortunate patients with services which may be able to assist, such as physiotherapy, rehabilitation and psychologists. For most busy intensivists, though, they are already stretched just dealing with the acute phase of the illness; most haven't the time or the inclination to establish post-hospital services for those they may have only treated for several days. They would also have to learn a whole set of different skills or familiarise themselves with the networks needed to manage the patient's chronic problems.

Post-traumatic stress disorder (PTSD) is a frequently used term but one that is difficult to define. It follows a traumatic event and is accompanied by an exaggeration of the usual suffering that people go through after such experiences. Instead of gradually decreasing with time, people with PTSD increasingly relive the event, accompanied by panic attacks and physical symptoms such as sweating and palpitations. Nobody knows exactly how many people suffer from PTSD as a result of admission to an intensive care unit. It could be as little as 5 per cent or perhaps as many as half of all patients.

The research that's emerging is frightening, especially for elderly patients. Up to half are re-admitted to hospital within six months, usually for an unrelated illness. Of those readmitted to hospital, only approximately 20 per cent of the elderly patients are alive one year later.

Severe infection is a common reason for being admitted to an intensive care unit. However, for the elderly frail, it is not the severity of their infection which influences outcome. We have become proficient at keeping people alive in intensive care. Their outcome is determined by factors such as their age, chronic health status and whether they had been admitted to hospital within the last six months. If you had minimal or moderate levels of frailty before hospitalisation, these may become severe disabilities after discharge. In other words, you cannot survive independently.

If you already had severe disabilities before hospitalisation, you have a high chance of dying or, at best, remaining severely disabled and having to be cared for in an institution. This is crucial information when considering what benefit there may be in admitting the elderly to a hospital and intensive care unit. However, this is rarely taken into account by the health system and the information is almost never shared with the patient and their carers.

What do we do in intensive care that causes patients to die and deteriorate so markedly after discharge? The problem with interpreting research of this sort is that the poor post-hospital outcomes are *associated* with being admitted to an intensive care unit, not necessarily *caused by* the intensive care unit admission.

This was not made clear in the research findings. The inference is that the patient's experience in the intensive care unit caused all the problems they suffered after leaving hospital. Much of the research concludes that we therefore need innovative 'interventions to accelerate recovery' or should aim to 'maintain function while treating acute illness'. The *Patient Protection and Affordable Care Act* in the United States has mandated that hospitals reduce readmissions of these elderly frail people. Maybe this organisation is on the right track, but it is for the wrong reasons.

The Act assumes that the hospital didn't deliver the appropriate treatment and the patient is returning with the same untreated condition. This may be the case sometimes. However, it is often related to the fact that the patients are coming to the end of their lives, that conventional medicine has little more to offer and that alternative ways of supporting them in the community should be encouraged.

Nevertheless, the focus on preventing readmissions is laudable. I suspect the Act is encouraging hospitals to put systems in place that would improve the patient's health status so they will not need rehospitalisation. In the eyes of authorities trying to correct the problems in health care, readmission rates are seen as a failure of the system. In another totally different way they may be correct.

Let me put a different spin on this research. Admission of elderly patients with a serious infection to an intensive care unit is a marker that this patient will deteriorate further, not as a result of the admission to the intensive care unit but as a natural part of the ageing process. The readmissions are not the result of a failure of the health system but a marker of natural and quite predictable deterioration in the health of elderly people. A different approach to management is required, including having honest discussions with people.

As an intensivist I feel proud that our specialty can treat these patients more effectively and that more will leave the hospital alive. But I would also like to see the picture from a patient's perspective. I want my specialty to be an integral part of the entire health system and to reassure myself that what I do will result in improvement to the patient's health and quality of life after they are discharged from hospital as well as feeling proud that the management of septicaemia within the four walls of the intensive care unit has improved over the years.

Similar research is beginning to emerge about other problems for which the elderly frail are admitted to intensive care units. For example, pneumonia, heart failure and heart attacks in the elderly frail are also associated with high readmissions to hospital and mortality rates. Most importantly, if the admission of an elderly frail person to an intensive care unit is a marker of decline in health, that person and their carer need to be informed so that their future planning can be based on good information. As it is, many are discharged from hospital with little information about what their future holds. Their state of health will deteriorate, requiring an increasing number of admissions to hospital, and the deterioration will become less amenable to improvement with conventional medicine.

The doctors involved in patients' care during the hospital admission see survival of the hospital experience as a triumph of modern medicine, not the beginning of a new and different state of health for the patient for which complex planning and support is required. Politicians and policy makers need to change the current health system in order to accommodate a different population of patients with different health challenges so that their choices can be accommodated according to their own wishes and not just face repeated hospitalisations and being subject to futile health interventions as their only option.

17

Knockin' on heaven's door

The topic of ageing and dying is generally kept at arm's length, but there are advantages to facing up to ageing and living rich and full lives in spite of its ravages. You still have the beauty of the natural world, the wonder of fellow human beings and the love you have for special people. Curiosity and imagination remain as you age. Humans, even old ones, can adapt to their changing brains, enabling them to hold on to their identity. It is conceivable that one can tap into latent and changing powers within the ageing brain.

Even when ageing merges with dying there is time for rational reflection and it's not always depressing.

Oliver Sacks, on learning he had a terminal condition in his early eighties, wrote in an opinion piece for *The New York Times*: 'I cannot pretend I am without fear. But my predominant feeling is one of gratitude. I have loved and been loved; I have been given much and I have given something in return; I have travelled and thought and written. I have had an intercourse with the world, a special intercourse of writers and readers. Above all, I have been a sentient being, a thinking animal, on this beautiful planet and that in itself has been an enormous privilege and adventure.'

Looked at in one way, elderly people are a burden. In developing countries, they represent one more mouth to feed and they need assistance in all sorts of ways to perform basic functions. There are societies where the elderly who had become a burden were taken to a snow-covered mountain and left to die of exposure. In other societies, the group just moved on without them. There are times when supporting the elderly compromises the survival of the younger members of the group. I'm sure there are many variations on these practices.

The equivalent to the snow-covered mountain in developed and so-called civilised societies is the subject of a thriving industry: retirement villages, nursing homes, old people's homes, aged care institutions. Whatever name you call them by, essentially they are where you send the elderly when they have become a burden, when they need increasing and sometimes full-time care which families may not be in a position to provide. There comes a point where our elderly require high maintenance to keep them safe and to tend to their basic needs.

The waiting lists are usually long and the expense for society or the individual is enormous. For those who can't afford the nursing home, there are often arguments among the children about who has to carry the majority of the burden.

Despite the efforts of well-meaning staff, aged care centres can be very sad places. You only have to see the residents sitting in sunrooms staring at walls or in a room blankly watching television. When a younger visitor walks in, especially ones with children, their faces light up and they stare expectantly, hoping for acknowledgement and a conversation.

Very few of us look forward to going into one of these institutions. The people about to be committed have probably committed other elderly people in the past. When the time comes, we are aware of the stigma and what is unsaid: that we are near the end of the line.

Many of the staff who work in these places are committed and provide excellent care. However, like the residents, many would like to be elsewhere. They are among the lowest paid in a society that pays lip service to the wonderful job the staff are doing: caring for their loved and valued elderly.

You might be able to delay the time when you can no longer survive without assistance, but you will inevitably become increasingly dependent. You might need only a small amount of assistance initially, but if you survive long enough you will eventually live a bed-bound existence. Many of the more enlightened institutions take this into account. You can move from a section offering low care to one where total care in a bed is needed.

Some of the features of ageing for which you may seek help from a doctor include falls, incontinence, loss of muscle bulk and strength, visual impairment, hearing impairment, delirium, frailty, malnutrition, immobility and chronic pain. Some of these conditions can be helped, such as with hearing aids or glasses.

Many others will inevitably become worse and not amenable to medical interventions.

In my own attempt to delay the inevitable I try to swim most days—about 600 metres. First, I couldn't get out of the pool without resorting to the steps, then I couldn't get into the pool gracefully without the steps. I can still put my pants and shoes on without sitting down but I'm starting to become unsteady and hop about trying to maintain my balance. It won't be long before I join those who slowly try to find each leg in the pants while sitting down.

The elderly are a testimony to the limitations of modern medicine, diets, exercise, herbal concoctions and lifestyle. For many of us during our lifetime, the beauty of nature is something we loved. It gave us sustenance and joy. At the same time, nature is stalking us, creeping up, causing our bodies to decay and, eventually, delivering the final blow.

Films and television series rarely star people in their sixties or older. Even when they do, they are usually portrayed as stereotypes, embedded somewhere in the nuclear family. (There are exceptions, of course, such as Clint Eastwood, who remains compelling in his late eighties.) If we are serious about crafting a new image for the elderly, it has to include the natural features of ageing but with a different spin; the usual stereotypes need to be challenged.

When I was visiting my mother in a nursing home, I would imagine a television series. It would begin with a group of elderly residents plotting an escape. They would seek collaboration from the outside world to assist in the getaway. The collaborators would include those who had similarly been rejected by society as 'useless'—for example, the young unemployed, whom the elderly would engage to assist them in getting around and driving. Once they had escaped, subsequent episodes would feature them evading recapture and coming up with complex schemes to regain control over their own finances.

There could be an episode based on revenging a scam inflicted on one of the gang by a financial adviser. Another episode would involve settling a score with a family member who had cheated one of the residents. The gang would seek out and punish perpetrators of elder abuse.

A special squad of elderly experts who had personal experience and know-how with exploitation of the aged would feature in the series. They would crack cases of financial abuse by those with 'inheritance impatience'. The revenge would be swift, ruthless and as complex as the best dramas. The baddies would be humiliated, publically shamed, cut out of the will and bankrupted. The squad's role would also be to uncover and follow up physical and psychological abuse and neglect.

The whole country would be alerted to possible sightings of the escapees and the close calls they had avoiding capture. There would be passionate pleas from family members on live broadcasts, worried about the escapees' health and whether they were continuing to take their pills—which of course they weren't and they had never felt better.

Maybe there could be an unexpected subplot based on a love story—after all, the elderly fall in love too. The show's writers and actors would mainly be the elderly. The program would be conceived and funded by the elderly. It would give them a voice and a new standing. Paparazzi would follow the main actors and the public would devour scandals. Actors would no longer be judged on their youth, looks and weight. The baby boomers, with their larger pulling power, may lead this sort of revolution.

There are many challenges in how we deal with ageing at a societal level. First and foremost, ageing needs to be normalised and integrated into the way we all live. Simply building more little rooms in institutions is not the answer. The aged deserve more than three meals a day and a television.

There is a German word, *Mehrgenerationenhauser*, which describes a place where many different age groups are housed on the same site. For example, childcare centres and youth drop-in centres are integrated with places that care for the elderly. The elderly are involved in childcare and the young help the elderly with their mobile phones and computers. This facilitates all sorts of interactions and helps to restore vanishing social networks.

Imagination and commitment is required. We need to be more outrageous, think outside the box and use our imagination to explore other options. The elderly, or those on the brink of old age, should be involved in coming up with the solutions.

Older people want to be needed. There must be many ways in which we could construct activities of living around the need to be needed in more imaginative ways than we currently do.

18

How to choose a good doctor and a good hospital

Ask any doctor how they would choose a doctor for themselves and they will say: 'Ask around.' Doctors would rarely use league tables or hard data to search for one—and they would certainly never rely on Dr Google. A search engine may be able to diagnose straightforward diseases, but most conditions are not straightforward. Medical conditions have to be considered in the context of the patient's personality, their past history, their living circumstances, their age and overall health status and many other factors which will influence not only the diagnosis but also how to manage it. A good physician is also a careful taker of a patient's history. The clinician will give weight to the story as being told by the person. They will also drill down on parts of the history that may give clues to the clinical problem.

Remember that doctors working in different areas will have different attributes. When I had neck surgery, I chose the best technician. His bedside manner left a bit to be desired, but who cares when someone is working with your spinal cord?

When assessing a doctor, remember they may be 'good' at certain things and not others. Certain of my colleagues in final-year medicine were top of the class for the whole six undergraduate years, but when it came to putting the theory into practice, they verged on being dangerous. Someone who can diagnose a rare disease from the list of the known diseases, rather than dealing with the unknown with acceptance and curiosity, sometimes defines a clever doctor. The same doctors who can make a rare diagnosis may find it difficult to live with the uncertainty of medical practice, of acknowledging that much of our practice is not underpinned by precise theory and science. There are many clusters of symptoms and signs, which, as yet, have no label. Many could handle that.

Others feel intimidated by the idea of abandoning all their learning and instead exploring the complaints of patients and going on a journey with them; a journey that has not as yet been neatly described in textbooks. It also means not abandoning the patient if their complaint doesn't fit into current teachings. It means being comfortable with uncertainty, being honest with the patient and, if nothing else, relieving pain and any other suffering while searching for more answers.

Some of those who didn't thrive in the area of clinical practice went into other specialties of medicine, such as epidemiology or administration, where different skills were needed. Even within the different specialties of clinical practice, a wide variety of skills are required for different areas of medicine. For example, the technical skills required for repairing injuries such as broken bones are different to those needed to manage an elderly patient with chronic health issues and inadequate support services. Even within a single specialty, such as surgery, a clinician may be better at the technical aspect of repair than relieving symptoms such as pain. Below are some of the attributes to consider when evaluating some of the different specialties in medicine. (This is aimed at elderly patients but there may be some relevant messages for others.)

The family practitioner is the key to managing elderly people where most want to be cared for: in their own home. Here is a list of important attributes, in no particular order: honesty with compassion; the ability to see your medical condition in the context of who you are in the bigger social picture; doesn't automatically prescribe pills for every condition; gives you a feeling of trust; discusses ageing and dying in a straightforward, practical way; does the routine things well, e.g. management of blood pressure and dispensing of lifestyle advice; not afraid to say, 'I'm not too sure' or 'I don't know but we'll go on a journey together—remembering that sometimes we will never know, but as much as possible I'll try to manage any symptoms in the meantime'; and will investigate and refer to others when necessary but not just for defensive medico–legal imperatives.

Oncologists and haematologists Beware. Their hearts are in the right place but they are programmed to 'cure' you, when more often than not, that is not possible, especially as you become older. Gravitate towards those who articulate the problem and offer some solutions but temper it with: 'However, at your age we need to balance the possibility of improvement with you suffering as a result of side effects and false hope.' The better ones will adjust their treatment options around your priorities in life and not around the latest chemotherapy regime. Remember the famous study which showed that patients who had chemotherapy and palliative care together lived longer and had a better quality of life than those who had chemotherapy alone.

Surgeons As an intensivist, I sometimes say to surgeons: 'It really hurts me to say this, but you work in a profession that can actually make people better or even cure them.' However, if you are elderly, you will not recover as fast, or perhaps not recover at all. You will be more likely to have serious complications, resulting in a much worse health state and decreased quality of life. Trust the surgeons who say, 'We could operate but I have serious misgivings about whether that will help you,' and then go on to explain not just the list of complications on the consent form but the surgery itself in the context of your current age and state of health and what, at best and at worst, it could offer. Then think about it, and then think again.

Geriatricians These doctors specialise in managing elderly people. In theory they are the appropriate physicians to care for the aged patient. Many of them are very competent, but beware if they tend to apply the usual conventional medical approach of pills and procedures. Trust the ones who discuss your 'illness' in the wider context of ageing and dying in an honest and compassionate way. Demand that their suggested treatment options are consistent with your priorities in life.

Palliative care Under the current way medicine operates you will not usually see a palliative care physician until the very end. They hover around the outer boundaries of medicine until one of their specialist colleagues, in the area of 'curative' (or perhaps, more accurately, 'keeping you alive') medicine, finally throws in the towel. But when you do encounter one, they could prevent you suffering pain and other unpleasant symptoms in the latter stages of your life and that is worth gold.

Be pre-emptive. If you suspect you are not responding to conventional treatment, ask your family practitioner or other treating doctors if they have considered palliative care. This is a crucial question which could sort out the better doctors. At the least, your treating doctor may take the opportunity to honestly discuss your prognosis with you. If they don't, push them hard. For example, say that you wouldn't see it as a failure on their behalf if conventional treatment played a decreasing role in your future health status. Explain that you've heard that there is increasing evidence that commencing palliative care early, together with conventional medicine, is becoming widely accepted. Doctors don't like to be considered to be out of touch.

Go on to explain that symptom control is as important to you as striving for a cure or improvement in health status. Beware of the doctor who, in answer to your question about palliative care, says: 'We are not there just yet.' Insist on being told what 'there' means exactly in terms of your prognosis and future health trajectory. Then, as your health decreases despite more conventional approaches, you have the option to fine-tune the balance between 'symptomatic treatment' and 'curative treatment'.

Avoid a palliative care physician who sees their role as only being involved when all conventional treatment has ceased.

In summary, it is difficult for a layperson to choose a good doctor. Ideally you need a service broker who knows who to contact in order to find the best doctor for each particular specialty, someone who has insider knowledge. This may not be possible and search engines are crude substitutes.

Assessing 'good' doctors using administrative and easily obtained information only gives a superficial picture of their qualities and attributes, such as whether they are registered and what qualifications they have. As with comparing hotels and restaurants on the internet, attempts at peer or patient ratings are prone to gaming and distortion. Moreover, they usually don't balance the different attributes that reflect your own priorities. For example, you wouldn't prefer a good bedside manner over technical skills in a specialty where technical skills will determine your outcome. Similarly, for a family practitioner, communication skills and bedside manner would be more important than technical skills if the family doctor carries out few technical interventions. Obviously, it would be ideal for each doctor to have all the skills associated with being 'a good doctor'.

You probably have almost as much to fear from the system within which doctors operate as from the doctors themselves. For example, fear of litigation can distort their ability to practise good medicine. The fact that doctors are trying to build their own careers while working within a bureaucracy whose goal is to reduce costs can distort the delivery of good care. And technology can introduce more risks than benefits.

Like doctors, different hospitals will have different strengths and weaknesses. Some may have an excellent emergency department service, where on presenting with an undifferentiated illness you will be rapidly assessed, your life-threatening situations dealt with, your symptoms attended to and then you will be triaged along an appropriate pathway.

On the other hand, there might be a parallel system in the same hospital for dealing with elective surgery and other procedures. By this time, you would have been sorted to a large degree and a decision has been made to perform the procedure. The technical proficiency of the proceduralist is probably the most important contributor to your outcome. However, your outcome will also depend on the anaesthetist, nursing staff, infection control and general support, such as pain relief. We are talking about a system here and your outcome will be judged on all of those aspects being synchronised and interacting appropriately.

The effectiveness of this system is almost impossible to evaluate. Almost certainly, some part of that system will work better than others. The whole may be evaluated by outcomes such as operative complications, wound infections, length of stay and mortality. However, many factors, not the least of which could be the patient's underlying health status, may contribute to a patient's outcome as much as the hospital environment itself.

Basically, there are several systems operating in parallel within the hospital. First, there is your immediate medical problem being handled by your admitting doctor and associated health professionals.

Then there is what could be described as the patient flow or support services. That is, the army of people who arrange your admission; assign a bed; give you meals; order stores and equipment; clean the hospital; and send you bills. Then there are the senior, mid-level and lower-level administrators whom you also pay for, either directly or indirectly through your taxes. It is difficult for you to judge what impact the latter people have on your health outcomes when choosing the best hospital as they are subject to different priorities, such as financial pressures and avoiding bad publicity.

The third and increasingly important stream influencing your outcome is a backup system operating across the whole hospital in case you unexpectedly deteriorate. Your own specialist doctor will almost never be able to perform that function. For a start, they cannot be in the hospital night and day. And they will almost certainly not have the skills, knowledge and experience to recognise and manage every possible medical emergency, even if they were near your bedside at all times. This is not a criticism of the admitting doctor. No one doctor can have the skills and knowledge to manage every possible emergency. Always check that your hospital has a rapid response or medical emergency team system. Check that the response is, indeed, rapid and is staffed by someone with advanced resuscitation skills.

While you can check that a nationally recognised group accredits a hospital, it doesn't necessarily reassure you that the hospital will deliver good care to you. Hospitals prepare for the accreditation visit like we do for a visit from the health minister. Walls are painted, files brought up to date and policies displayed and made available in easily accessible places. Managers, who a week earlier could be threatening and finding ways to cut funding, will suddenly be interested in patient care. They will proudly introduce staff they had never met previously to the accreditation visitors and make fine speeches to the hospital staff after being successfully accredited for a further few years.

How do you judge a good hospital? Quality of care depends mainly on the team of direct healthcare deliverers. You need to evaluate good teamwork—but that is almost impossible. Moreover, it depends on what you want from the hospital: elective surgery? Complex investigations? Sophisticated interventions? Or attending the emergency department with an undifferentiated illness? Hospitals are extremely complex and their quality of care is difficult to judge. Moreover, your choice may be limited by your geographical location and ability to pay.

Comparing doctors on the basis of mortality may be misleading, as it would largely depend on the type of patients being selected. The death of a twenty-year-old having a minor orthopaedic procedure is a rare event and one that would require serious investigation. Deaths in older patients having the same operation mightn't be as significant, depending on how ill they were before the operation. Heart surgery on otherwise healthy young patients would have a better outcome than in elderly patients with multiple chronic conditions. On the other hand, in view of the high risks, maybe the latter patients shouldn't be having major surgery.

Choosing a good hospital is even more difficult than choosing a good doctor and the choice will be based on multi-dimensional attributes, of which gourmet meals and a private room should probably come last. As with choosing a good doctor, you could ask around. In the case of elective procedures, the choice could be largely determined by where the good doctor is working. Then it's in the lap of the gods.

19

The medicalisation of grieving

I grew up in the south of Sydney in beautiful bushland sloping down to the deep waterfront of Yowie Bay. We built a house there in 1954, financed by my father's war service loan of £3000 over fifty years at a notional and almost negligible interest rate—a reward for serving his country. The block of land, which was to be worth millions many years later, was a wedding gift from my grandfather. His father, in turn, had built a fishing shack on it over fifty years earlier.

No one wanted to live in the Sutherland Shire at that time. It was frontier territory. When we moved there from the inner city, it was like moving to the middle of nowhere. Gradually, though, I made new friends, one of whom was my next-door neighbour, Peter Mills, who opened my eyes to the secrets of the land and the beauty of the bay. We remained close until the end of high school, when we went our separate ways. I didn't see him again until many years later, when he contacted me out of the blue. I arranged to have breakfast in a cafe with Pete and his wife, Barb.

We had a delightful time reminiscing (hopefully not boring Barb too much) before turning to more recent events in our lives. They showed me pictures of their daughter and new grandson—Sean Hamish. Then Peter produced a picture of their son, Hamish, taken many years ago, just before he died at the age of fourteen. He had suddenly arrested from a rare cardiac condition while he and Pete were working together in the back-yard. Peter's eyes filled with tears as he described what had happened to their handsome, happy boy.

Pete and Barb both worked in the health industry at the time: Barb as a nurse and Pete as an anatomist. But what it is like to attempt to resuscitate your own son and then come to terms with his death is probably not something you can even begin to understand unless you've been through it. Pete finally picked the picture up and said, 'Children shouldn't die before their parents.'

Around that time, I read in a medical journal about an illness known as 'complicated grief', one of many new 'diseases' that acquired names and doubtless many PhD dissertations and medical scholars all scrambling to define some original area of research and make their mark.

'Complicated grief' has characteristics which distinguish it from 'normal grief'. 'Complicated grief' is also known as 'prolonged grief disorder'. It is defined as 'intense grief that lasts longer than expected, according to social norms'. Now there is a statement that begs questions. What the hell are these 'social norms' and how do these experts acquire their knowledge? This sort of abnormal grief usually occurs after the loss of a 'romantic partner' or child, the journal stated. What the hell is a 'romantic partner'? I leave it to Monty Python and your own imagination . . . The hallmark of 'complicated grief' is persistent intense yearning, longing and sadness, but it does diminish with time, apparently—much like 'normal' grief.

Believe it or not, there is science around this condition. It is suggested by these experts that there are changes in the brain that are visible during magnetic resonance imaging (MRI) when people think about grieving. We have pictures, therefore it must be real. If we put Pete and Barb in an MRI and showed them a picture of Hamish, something would light up on the machine. If we put a hundred such people in the MRI and show them similar reminders—voila!— we have a PhD and several publications. What ethics committees would have allowed such emotional torture to be inflicted in order to put a name on grief—a response which is such a normal part of every human's make-up?

We see many elderly people who grieve over the death of their partner; at the time of their death, of course, but also after many months or years when apparently it is abnormal and assumes a disease status.

As a rule, people over the age of seventy who attempt suicide are serious about not wanting to live. Albert was eighty-eight years of age when he took an overdose of a morphine solution and twenty-five sleeping tablets. He had no idea what quantity was needed to guarantee death so he took every bit of medication he could get his hands on. It was twelve months to the day his wife had died. He was living with his daughter, who found him unconscious in his bedroom and immediately called the ambulance. The paramedics reversed the effect of the morphine with a drug called naloxone. Before the naloxone, his breathing had almost ceased; he was deeply unconscious and his heart was on the verge of stopping. After the naloxone, he was able to be roused and his breathing and pulse rate picked up. Albert was put on an oxygen mask for the trip to the hospital's emergency department. His life had been saved; he was out of danger. What should we do with him now?

Albert was in the system. The first thing the system does is to make sure he remains alive. This is easy. The effects of morphine and sleeping tablets, when discovered early enough, are benign and easily managed. Albert didn't even need to be on a breathing machine. He was sitting in the emergency department, drowsy but otherwise stable. Despite his drowsiness, Albert's mood vacillated between sadness and anger. His attempt to die had failed. He was close to his daughter, who was in tears and holding his hand. But nothing could remove Albert's sadness and loneliness as a result of his wife's death, his friend of nearly seventy years. He was concerned about his daughter's distraught state but angry that he'd lost possibly his only chance at doing the job right.

The system now classified Albert as being at 'risk of suicide'. He had to be monitored carefully. Because his daughter worked full time and would not be able to watch him continuously, he would have to be institutionalised. Decisions had already been made about what sort of institution he would need to be placed in. He had lost his wife and now he could no longer live with his daughter, nor share the life and distractions of his two grandchildren.

Psychiatrists do not like to visit intensive care units. They're not too sure what to do with patients who are unconscious or drowsy as a result of having a life-threatening 'illness'. The psychiatrist's opinions are almost invariably along the lines of: 'Requires further assessment when the patient's clinical condition has improved and should be prescribed antidepressants in the meantime.'

Many patients who attempt suicide are not medically depressed. They are simply sad, without hope, and choose in a rational way to die rather than face the daily unrelenting bleakness of life. Such was the case with Albert. He didn't want to live anymore; he had experienced twelve months of grief after losing his wife. Time was not making things better, only worse. When I saw him, he was totally rational and simply did not want to live any longer. He was eighty-eight years old and had lived a good life; he just didn't want to keep living without his wife. The choice to end his life was understandable and, in my opinion, a normal reaction. He just didn't know how to do it properly. I hasten to add that there are many suicide prevention groups whose admirable work has saved many lives, allowing people to embrace the second chance they had been given—especially younger people who had been facing a crisis of one sort or another. But Albert's despair was rational and well founded. I don't believe this deeply embedded sadness is a medical condition.

The psychiatric review and the clinical notes accurately documented his life. Born in Scotland, Albert's mother died of diphtheria when he was seven years old; he had a rough childhood. The family moved around a lot and he was looked after by various relatives. He joined the British army when he was seventeen and fought in Europe during the Second World War. He and his wife migrated to Australia when he was thirty years old. He had no significant medical illness and disliked doctors. Albert had smoked until eight years ago and drank regularly until his late seventies. The psychiatrist also noted that he was pleasant and totally lucid, but because he was 'depressed' and voiced a 'death wish' there was a high risk of self-harm. He certainly was at risk of self-harm if that meant a further attempt at suicide. The issue was why and how we were to prevent it.

Was Albert medically depressed or was he normally depressed or grieving or sad? Was his sadness a normal reaction to personal anguish with no hope of cure (after all, we couldn't bring his wife back)? How were we to treat his condition? We would have to watch over him twenty-four hours a day. For how long? Until he came to his senses? Until time cured him? Until the antidepressants kicked in? It was hard to know.

For the time being his sadness had been converted to a medical condition with a name: depression. As night follows day, he was given medical treatment: an antidepressant. Next he had to be transferred to an institution where he could be 'watched carefully'.

The geriatricians examined him and concluded he was not demented; he was rational. As well as being rational it was decided he was physically independent. However, he was not allowed out of bed due to the risk of a fall. Our hospital had seen an increase in the number of falls over the last three months, making the incidence of falls higher than the benchmark—the average for the state—and this set alarm bells ringing in the bureaucracy. The solution was to confine all patients over the age of eighty to their beds. The system had dealt another blow to Albert; he became even sadder. He already felt like a burden and now he wasn't allowed to walk around, even with a guard.

A week later he was sent to a psychogeriatric unit. He was certainly old, so probably geriatric, but the 'psycho' bit didn't seem to apply to Albert. His grief seemed decidedly uncomplicated and easily understood to me.

I sometimes wonder what happened to Albert. Did he manage to take the right dose without being caught?

⌐

After careful consideration, the members of the World Health Organization's Working Group on the

Classification of Disorders Specifically Associated with Stress recommended that 'prolonged grief disorder' become a disease and be published in the *International Classification of Diseases 11th Revision*. It is currently undergoing field testing, perhaps in cafes like the one where Pete and Barb showed me the picture of Hamish, so a PhD student in the course of their studies may observe Pete's eyes welling up more than twenty-five years after his son's death and assign him to their cohort of diseased persons.

The disease is now being presented to the working group for the fifth edition of the *Diagnostic and Statistical Manual of Mental Disorders (DSM-5)* and is an official entity called 'persistent complex bereavement disorders'.

A more relevant question may be what are these 'current social and cultural norms' outside of which you have a disease—a disease defined by a group of academics? And what qualifies them to define what they consider to be 'norms'? Where, I would ask, is the evidence?

Even more bizarre and dangerous is the concept that once you have a disease, a treatment must follow. In the case of prolonged grief disorder, it is either psychotherapy or pharmacotherapy. Let's be grateful that it's not lobotomy or electroconvulsive therapy. The treatment is recommended as early as six months after the death of the patient's loved one. Another medical industry is about to be created. As if it's not cruel enough that we are more often than not dying in a medicalised way, we are now also being robbed of the right to grieve in whatever way we feel is appropriate.

20

The taboos of ageing, death and dying

Ageing, death and dying are the new taboos. We only talk about them in hushed tones, as if they weren't inevitable. Like sex in the nineteenth century, ageing takes place behind closed doors and not in polite circles. It happens, but we only refer to it in clichéd terms and with lame attempts at humour.

Nelson Mandela spent most of the last year of his life in hospitals suffering futile attempts to stave off the inevitability of ageing, which gradually merges with dying. Of all the men in the world who could face the truth if it had been explained in an honest and straightforward way, with dignity and acceptance, it was Nelson Mandela. There is a massive industry devoted to the denial of ageing, peddling anti-ageing creams, tablets, operations and lifestyle. But it seems ridiculous not to acknowledge that it will still occur, as will dying and death—in many cases as a result of ageing eventually catching up with us. So let's start talking about it; not to make ourselves sad and depressed but to integrate ageing, dying and death into our everyday lives in an honest and realistic way. We shouldn't feel ashamed or embarrassed as we watch our bodies age and silently contemplate dying.

The taboo of ageing, death and dying became startlingly apparent when in 2009 the United States attempted to overhaul its health system under President Obama. Included in the proposal for a new system was a provision to reimburse doctors for discussing end-of-life issues with patients. As I have explained in previous chapters, the American system is largely based on a fee for service. In other words, doctors are paid for doing things. The more they do, the more they are paid. It is not surprising, therefore, that elderly patients near the end of life are admitted to hospitals and, from there, into intensive care units where they are put on life support machines and subjected to expensive interventions in their last few days or weeks of life. Doctors are paid to do things *to* patients, not necessarily to do things *for* them. Under this system, there is a generous payment for prolonging life in the face of futility and, in comparison, no recompense for taking the time to sit down with patients and their caregivers.

Obama's new system was to correct this by paying doctors to discuss end-of-life plans with patients over a one-hour period. It was only a fraction of what would be paid for medical procedures or interventions, but it was a start. The plan simply proposed to reimburse doctors for discussing the patient's wishes around options such as advanced care directives. This is not unreasonable as more than 70 per cent of people want to die at home.

The old system benefited large pharmaceutical companies, doctors and all those who delivered private health care. It was not designed around the needs of patients and their carers. The proposed reforms would have threatened the profits of these industries. A widespread and expensive campaign was mounted against the reforms, funded by those who were to gain from the status quo.

A killer blow (excuse the pun) was delivered by Sarah Palin, a Republican former governor of Alaska, who used the words 'death panel' to criticise the plan. The label took on a life of its own. Opponents described the reimbursement as a vicious assault on the elderly, claiming that its aim was to tell people how to end their lives and that it would lead to government-sponsored euthanasia, with panels of faceless bureaucrats deciding who was to live and who was to die. Seniors were to be put to death by governments and comparisons were made with Nazi Germany. It was ironic that in the 'land of the free' patients and their caregivers were to be denied what arguably would be one of the more important discussions of their lives. Choices about the way they were to die would remain in the hands of those with vested interests. The individual's rights and choices were dictated by people who profited from the aged.

Apart from the industries that would lose by the proposed amendments to health care in the United States, it was also an unwelcome reminder of the inevitability of death. It challenged the widespread belief that the miracles of modern medicine would neutralise the threat of ageing and dying. The consultation payments were removed from the bill. The phrase 'death panel' had almost derailed the whole bill and all of its other reforms.

It is not only in the United States that the prospect of dying triggers emotional reactions largely based on fear. The Liverpool Care Pathway (LCP) for the Dying Patient, developed in the city of Liverpool in the United Kingdom, is perhaps the most widely cited and accepted example of managing end-of-life care in the world. It was designed to recognise that people do die and to create a specifically designed program allowing the terminally ill a peaceful, dignified and symptom-free death.

Unfortunately, thanks in large part to a sensation-alised media campaign, the plan was scrapped. One report claimed that a terminally ill patient had been placed on the Liverpool Care Pathway without his wife's knowledge and that he was being deprived of food and water. It seems to have been a failure of both communication and resources necessary to operate the system as much as the system itself. The Liverpool Care Pathway aimed to provide a pain-free and dignified death, but it was essential that this be explained in an honest and sensitive way. Apparently this may not have happened, and that is a serious failure of the system. Implementing the plan required education, training, infrastructure and widespread support. Without these resources it should come as no surprise that busy bedside clinicians focused more on conventional management of patients on the general wards of a hospital rather than attempting to implement a complex plan such as the Liverpool Care Pathway.

The media frenzy sparked by the Liverpool Care Pathway was similar to that sparked in the United States by the alleged 'death panel'. In irresponsible hands, the topic of dying and death can create conflict, fear and sensation. Many in the media mischievously misrepresented the Liverpool Care Pathway in order to cause as much of a splash as possible. There was not much in the way of a careful and balanced argument that the terminally ill had rights and that dying should not be exploited for the wrong reasons, let alone that people at the end of life deserve specialised and sensitive care.

My team at the University of New South Wales is developing a way of predicting the end-of-life course for elderly frail patients. The test is called Criteria for Screening and Triaging to Appropriate aLternative care (CriSTAL) and is based on answers to routine questions asked as part of the medical history, as well as simple measurements of physiological function such as blood pressure and pulse rate. It also includes ways of measuring the underlying state of health of the patient. We believe its main strength is that it could be used in a practical way at the bedside. Even at this early stage the most important predictors are the age of the patient and their degree of frailty (see chapter 11).

When details of the test were first published, even as a theoretical concept, we were exposed to the same sensational media coverage as the Liverpool Care Pathway. The evaluation tool we were developing was seen as a 'death test'. Interestingly, if the patient was twenty-three years old and had a brain tumour for which there was no treatment, the first question that patient would ask is: 'How long have I got?' For the hypothetical young patient with the brain tumour, the CT scan and biopsy were not 'death tests'; they were crucial indicators of the patient's prognosis. It would be inconceivable that the results of these tests would be kept secret. The implications of knowing that you may only have a year or so to live are vital to the patient and their caregivers. The patient with the brain tumour would be allowed to know the terminal nature of their condition and, acknowledging the enormous grief involved, would be allowed to plan their own way of facing and dealing with dying. Armed with similar prognostic information about an elderly frail person, I believe we have a similar obligation to share this information. It is no more a 'death test' in an elderly frail person near the end of life than it is for the twenty-three-year-old cancer patient. Armed with information, the next step in our research will be to empower patients and their carers to make their own choices about how they want to live the remainder of their life. It may be that the elderly frail would still want to undergo repeated hospitalisation and complex interventions and to spend their last few days or weeks on a ventilator in an intensive care unit. Or it may be that they would want to spend their time at home as long as appropriate services were available to ensure they did not suffer too much and that their caregivers were supported by professionals and could access services such as respite care.

The system is intuitive: recognise elderly people who may not have long to live; have honest and empathetic discussions with them; and empower them to consider their own preferences about how they wish to spend that time. The implementation of such a system did not involve unravelling genes, developing expensive drugs or using complex interventions. It has nothing to do with the billions spent on medical IT systems which promise but rarely deliver a substantiated improvement in patient care and outcomes. In spite of an increasingly technological approach to medicine, there is still a place for listening to what people are saying and facilitating involvement in their own health and lifestyle choices.

To give patients and their caregivers choices fulfils all of the aspirations of a democratic and caring society. To deny patients choice is the real threat to independence.

The subject of ageing, death and dying needs to be brought out into the open. There will be all sorts of benefits for us individually and as a society. There would be less guilt and more transparency when discussing options for the people we love who are becoming old and frail. There would be less reluctance to involve the elderly frail in discussions and choices. Hopefully, these discussions would be conducted earlier in people's lives and, of course, be flexible and open to change as ageing occurred.

The current costs of managing these people in acute hospitals could be diverted to support them in ways that they wanted. At the same time, it is important to avoid using cost as the major driver. It's about providing excellent community support, consistent with people's choices. This may also coincide with considerable savings in health care—a win–win situation.

21
Where to next?

It's crept up on us and we've been slow to adapt. While we are inundated with medical miracles on a daily basis, the health system is failing to meet its major challenge. We are getting older. Not only have medical miracles had very little impact on ageing but the whole health system is constructed around the way we did things over a hundred years ago.

Hospitals gradually became the self-proclaimed flagships of modern health care. That's where all the technology and clever people are and where advanced medicine that makes a real difference is practised. Family practitioners now operate around the edges of health care, not at the centre. They are encouraged to refer their patients to specialists whenever there is a problem of any significance.

The health system was built around younger people with a single problem or diagnosis. Medicine has divided itself up according to the area of the body where the affliction may be occurring; the heart, lungs, brain, gut, bones and joints all have specialists claiming that territory. Their years of training, the textbooks they read, the journals they study, the conferences they attend, the colleagues they mix with all belong to the same organ or confined area of medicine. Their professional and governing bodies are also divided along these rigid lines. Research is confined more and more to esoteric aspects of that organ and the media tag along, reporting the new life-saving breakthroughs.

In the meantime, the population of our patients has radically changed, almost unnoticed by the traders in medical miracles. The majority of patients in hospitals are now over the age of seventy, many much older and many at the end of life.

The hospitals are antiquated institutions divided into fiefdoms, according to old rules.

It's a bit like the Polish cavalry waiting for the German invasion in 1939. The Poles' military intelligence didn't tell them that a different sort of military machine was about to invade their country: rapidly moving and well-organised troops; tanks; artillery pulled by trucks, not horses; and high performing aircraft supporting the invasion by bombing and strafing. It was all over in days.

Similarly, there is an invasion of the elderly in ambulances, overwhelming the emergency departments and being admitted to hospitals constructed according to the single-diagnosis principle, in which wards are divided first into 'medical' and 'surgical' and then subdivided into areas of the body. Thus medical specialists with a single area of expertise find themselves treating elderly patients with multiple age-related problems, all interacting in complex ways and most not influenced by our medical miracles.

Even geriatricians have not geared up to the new population of patients. They come from the same stable of training as the organ specialists: they are programmed to make you better. It's almost as if they've sworn an oath not to discuss dying. Nor are they allowed to say to a patient: 'Look, it may just be that you are getting older.' That would be an admission of defeat. So more tests are done, increasing numbers of tablets are dispensed and even major operations are contemplated.

There are exceptions, of course—geriatricians who don't mind pointing out that the emperor may have few clothes. James Goodwin from the University of Texas is one such exception. In his 1999 article 'Geriatrics and the Limits of Modern Medicine' he wrote: 'I have come to believe that modern medicine does not work well for old people.' He went on to observe: 'Overtreatment of 50-year-olds is mainly a matter of inconvenience and waste, whereas overtreatment of 80-year-olds borders on assault.' He urged his colleagues to reflect on the way their own parents and other loved ones are dying: over-treated, subject to futile operative procedures and put on life-support machines, and to remember that most doctors would not choose this way of dying and yet still inflict it on their patients.

Sadly, his appeal does not seem to have influenced our practice of applying medical miracles, designed to make people better, in increasingly perverse and futile ways, often causing pain and torture in the last few weeks of elderly people's lives.

There are other voices which, in my mind, should have alerted our society and medical specialists to the problems inherent in current modes of health care, and the serious consequences that may result.

For example, almost one-third of all urgent calls to doctors in hospitals are to the bedside of elderly patients at the end of their lives—not because of medical problems that can be cured, but because these patients are just normally and naturally dying. And for those elderly patients who survive the hospital experience, half die of old age within twelve months. Many of those unfortunate people suffer symptoms similar to post-traumatic stress disorder as a result of the hospital experience.

These are sobering facts. Not only can't we cure old age or even make a dent in it with modern medicine, but we are causing suffering to these people and their loved ones through futile interventions. For all of their technological advances and highly skilled staff, hospitals cannot recognise people at the end of life.

Ironically, most doctors acknowledge this issue in the corridors and at meal breaks during conferences; many have had similar experiences with their own relatives. But research in this area, one of the more important in our society, is almost non-existent. And what research there is often is simply manipulating large databases but with no knowledge of the way health care operates at the clinician–patient interface. The researchers are situated in offices crunching numbers, looking for random correlations which will point to a problem for someone else to address. They are divorced from clinical reality and have no idea of solutions nor access to answers. Fortunately, health research is moving away from defining the problem in yet more ways and, instead, moving towards implementing and evaluating interventions which address problems.

So where do we go from here? A predictable medical solution would be to medicalise dying in the elderly even further and to have all those at the end of life referred to palliative care specialists. At first glance, this might appear like a caring and realistic option: when medicine fails, bring in the palliative care specialists.

In fact, this may not be a realistic option. There would not be enough palliative care resources in the world to care for every elderly person near the end of life. Moreover, the specialty of palliative care is aimed at ensuring people do not suffer as they die. As a result, palliative care has successfully alleviated suffering and pain on a wide scale. However, most elderly people at the end of their life are not suffering pain and unpleasant symptoms. Their needs are not medical. They want to be treated in a place of their choosing; they don't want to be lonely; they need access to friends and family; they need help to retain some level of mobility; they need to be cleaned and have meals provided; they need their dignity and pride. These are not medical challenges.

Currently we spend at least AUD$1500 each day for a standard hospital bed and more than $4000 a day for treatment in an intensive care unit. The very best round-the-clock treatment could be provided for a fraction of that cost in the community.

The future is about redesigning our health system in a radical way. Most of those requiring health care are elderly. Much of the conventional treatment they currently receive is inappropriate, futile and not consistent with either the patient's wishes or their carer's. Moreover, this treatment is the major contributor to the unsustainable cost of our health system.

So let's ask the elderly what they want and, just as importantly, what they don't want, then design a caring and supportive system around *their* needs.

Acknowledgements

Many people have assisted me in the preparation of this book. My schooldays friend Peter Mills and his wife, Barbara, allowed me to tell the story of their son. My sister-in-law's family, especially Paul and Julie, allowed me to document Denise's final months of life. A thankyou to James Burrell, who gave me great advice on dementia. I'm particularly grateful to my colleagues with whom I've had many inspiring discussions over the years. A thankyou to all the staff at Allen & Unwin and my agent, Margaret Connolly, who constantly encouraged me and helped craft the book into its final form.

Finally, a special thankyou to my friend Sue Williams and my wife, Bobbi Ballas, who simultaneously inspired me and kept me on the straight and narrow.